UNLOCKING LEADERSHIP

UNLOCKING LEADERSHIP

UNLEASH YOUR POTENTIAL FOR PERSONAL AND BUSINESS SUCCESS

SYLVIA BURBERY

A&Co.

First published in Great Britain in 2025
by Authors & Co.
www.authorsandco.pub

Copyright © Sylvia Burbery 2025

Sylvia Burbery asserts the moral right to be identified as the
author of this work in accordance with the Copyright, Designs
and Patents Act 1988.

ISBN 978-1-917623-05-6 (paperback)
ISBN 978-1-917623-06-3 (hardback)

CONTENTS

INTRODUCTION

Why should you read this book? That's a good question. You are driven, ambitious and already equipped with a solid foundation of the functional, technical and business skills that have helped you to make it this far. Your success so far is just the beginning. Herein lies the hidden danger – the further you progress, the less those skills, on their own, are enough. In today's fast-paced, complex world, a new set of leadership skills has become critical.

You are at a crossroads: now is the time to set the course for the person you want to be, and the legacy you want to leave. You have huge potential and a huge choice: do you want to become a leader who looks back at the end of your career and reflects on the people you have developed, the relationships you have built, the different interests you have forged and the results you have delivered with and through others; or do you want to look back on the business success you have driven, but a success that is littered with the bodies you have trampled on, the relationships you have broken.

You value your family, friends and loved ones but may be struggling to balance all the demands on you. Do you want to be one of those unfortunate souls who eventually retire, lonely and without friends or outside interests, often only to die prematurely?

You may be thinking, "I would never do that," and I know you have the best intentions. I have also seen how easy it is for people to fall into the trap of focusing only on their business results. You may think I am being a bit melodramatic or extreme. Surely those sorts of things only happen in fiction – think *Citizen Kane* or *The Wolf of Wall Street*. The characters in those stories might be extreme, but they resonate because they are plausible and reflect the sad reality for many people.

Success can drive success; it can also raise expectations – your own and those of the people around you. That can lead to stress and a tendency to double down on the business fundamentals that you know will work. Even with the very best of intentions to make good, balanced business and management decisions it is easy to misstep. But it doesn't have to be this way. There is another way to lead – without compromising on results. With empathy and vulnerability, you can maximise the performance of those around you, deliver consistent, exceptional results, and live a fulfilling and rounded life.

Over my thirty-five years in leadership, I have learned, often through my mistakes, how to unleash unrealised potential and deliver exceptional results for yourself and for the people around you. This happens when you put your energy and focus into bringing your whole self to everything you do, and when you create the conditions that encourage others to do the same. Those that don't embrace the human side of leadership risk losing themselves, burning out, alienating those around them and most importantly missing out on the fulfilment of seeing others exceed what they thought was even possible. When we unleash the full potential of those around us our results will follow.

Often there is a tendency to put your focus on the business first and plan to address the 'soft people stuff' when you have time. Too often, this means the people can get missed altogether. My experience, and the experience of others I have coached, has been that focusing on people and strengthening those so-called soft skills, leads to long-lasting, sustainable success. The people around us have amazing capacity and you face the trap of missing this if you haven't learned how to lead in a way that encourages, supports and enables them to fully unlock that capacity.

It is unfortunate that right at the time our careers are taking off, we often also experience the competing demands of raising children or supporting elderly parents, and our peers, colleagues and team members are often struggling with the same dilemmas. We look for the magic bullets that will make it easier. We tell ourselves that we are the strong ones who can make it through successfully and we pretend we can also carry everyone around us. We tend to prioritise the immediate, the obvious and the most demanding and forget to nurture the relationships that will sustain us. This may work in the short term but the consequences can be devastating in the long term – for you, for the people around you, and for your business endeavours.

I don't claim to have all the answers, and I certainly don't claim to have gotten all this right the first time – in fact, this book is the result of the many, many learnings I have gleaned and continue to glean every day. I have had a successful leadership career in a large, multinational organisation, having had the privilege of living in five different countries and working across six continents, and with many diverse cultures. I have led, mentored and coached hundreds of people and have raised two children, with all the challenges parenthood entails, to successful independence. I am now in a happy and fulfilling relation-ship, enjoying the benefits of a blended family and the joys of grandparenting. I have learned some very valuable lessons along the way.

I have often been asked to share some of my reflections and learnings and for this reason, I humbly set out to write this book. You will find it filled with stories, tips and (hope-fully) provocations – not about business per se – but about the art of being human and treating those around you as human beings; about embracing vulnerability and about sitting with the discomfort of other people's vulnerability and emotions. This mastering of the art of being human leads to strong business outcomes. I firmly believe that those so-called 'soft skills' are the most important skills we can develop.

Back in 2012, I was in my second General Manager role, running a fairly sizable business in Australia. I had achieved success in my first General Manager role, driving a major transformation, and had started strongly in my new role too. But a couple of years in we started to struggle. The things that had worked well for me in a smaller business were less effective in the new context and I was trying to make sense of it.

I engaged a business consultant to help us diagnose the challenges we were facing in the business. We embarked on a series of interventions, one being to focus on our leadership impact. I was extremely clear about the type of impact I wanted to have as a leader. I believed passionately in empowering others and delivering results collectively. My management team and I all completed leadership impact assessments. You might think this was a time to double down on the business side of things, but I felt strongly that focusing on leadership and people would be our key unlocker.

We first completed a survey outlining the impact we wanted to have, then got 360-degree feedback on the impact we were actually having. This feedback was presented in the form of a circumflex, a circular graph with three colours: blue, which showed you were creating a positive, constructive impact; red, which indicated you were creating an aggressive environment; and green, which meant you were creating a passive-aggressive environment. There is plenty of data to show that leaders who create a strong, constructive (blue) impact consistently deliver better business results.

We were all together at an offsite meeting when the consultant shared our results with us. I cannot adequately express how devastated I felt when I received my feedback. I had hoped to see a graph in which blue dominated. I had always intended to have a positive impact on the team. This was certainly the case with the graph showing my desired impact, which was almost entirely blue. My actual impact, though, was very different, showing only a tiny bit of blue and lots of red and green. Glancing around the room at my team, who I thought were the problem, I could see that their results were a lot bluer than mine. I knew the consultant was going to ask who wanted to share their results, and that as I was the leader of the team, he expected me to share mine first.

All I could do at the time was stand up, share and own my results, tell the team how devastated I was, that I needed time to process them, and, most importantly, that I was committed to improving. I knew I needed to lead from the front, and this was not the time for defensiveness or avoidance. As much as I was embarrassed, confused and dismayed by my feedback, I also knew that this was my opportunity to set the tone for the team. No matter how good anyone's feedback was, there was always room for improvement. I realised that I had the opportunity to role model how to take the feedback and act on it.

This was, without a doubt, one of the most pivotal moments of my leadership career – one of my crossroads, if you like. The work I did next set me on a path of self-discovery and personal growth that has had a lasting positive impact on my professional and personal life.

Why do I share this now? Because I was extremely clear on the type of leader I wanted to be and thought I was. I had received glowing feedback throughout my career and had always been seen as someone with a lot of potential. I was starting to back myself and believed I could handle any challenge. That is why the results of the feedback were so devastating.

Knowing the theory, and even passionately believing in it, was very different from putting it into practice, especially in a larger business where it was impossible to have good, trusting relationships with every person. Without that feedback and some very good follow-up coaching and support, my career and in fact, my life, would have been very different. I am forever grateful for the insights and for the support of my team and my coach. I later shared the results with all ±1,500 employees in the business, along with my commitment to improve and the action plan I had developed.

You might already have it all together. You may be an excellent people leader. You may have your life in balance and be successfully juggling the multiple conflicting priorities you face. Hopefully, you will not have to face something quite as devastating as this was for me. Chances are, though, that things may not be quite as good as you think. No matter how good we are there is always room to improve. We never know when something will knock us, and we all have our 'shadow-side', that part that shows up when we are under stress or pressure. Even our strengths, when overused, can become a challenge. And this can easily undermine our success and the success of those around us.

At its core, this book is about being human and embracing our humanness, with all our strengths, our failures and our weirdness. You are a unique individual and all the people you work with are also unique human beings. We can so easily get caught up in the corporate context of 'managing talent' that we forget to nurture the human side. This can be a big miss. Treating ourselves and others as unique and precious individuals has, for me, unlocked a huge awareness of diversity and the unique gifts we all have. When people are truly seen and valued, they are able to bring their gifts to the fore, and magic can happen.

Through stories and anecdotes, both from my own experiences and from people I've coached, I will share some of the key, easily implemented ideas that have helped us to improve relationships at work and at home, to overcome challenges and to sustain success. While this book will focus on the 'softer', human side of leadership, I do not intend to imply any lack of value in the 'hard' business skills. You will by now have developed some functional/ technical expertise and a good understanding of how your business works. The business skills you have developed are valuable and valid and will continue to be important foundations for your success. Continually stretching your perspective and developing your critical thinking capability will also be important. But these skills on their own will not be enough.

My journey has been one of continuous growth and discovery. Through curiosity, vulnerability and a relentless thirst for feedback, I continue to strive to be the best version of my authentic self that I can. Through sharing my story and some of my key leadership and personal learnings I hope you glean some insights that help you to maximise your impact and become an even better version of *your* authentic self.

NB: While I believe this book is helpful to leaders in any context, my experience has been almost entirely in a large multinational environment. My stories and suggestions will no doubt reflect this. Take what is relevant to your context.

CHAPTER ONE
KNOWING YOURSELF

"Knowing yourself is the beginning of all wisdom."

– Aristotle

Knowing yourself is absolutely fundamental if you are going to maximise your potential and lead with real authenticity. When you know what is important to you – that is, when you can articulate your values, your priorities and your boundaries – you can define your purpose. This allows you to lead with consistency and in a way that is entirely congruent with who you are. Knowing your strengths, what energises you, the things you are not so good at, and the things you strongly dislike doing, helps you define the organisations you want to work for and the roles that will give you the most satisfaction. When you do work you love that plays to your strengths, you are far more likely to deliver sustainable success.

If you are already rolling your eyes and thinking this isn't for you, I can relate. When I was starting out in my career and I was asked to define my values, I cringed. It all seemed very introspective and required me to stop and reflect, and I wasn't particularly good at it. I didn't understand how knowing my values would make me or the business more successful. I was happy enough to receive feedback and was always keen to try and be better, but I didn't have a North Star to guide me. I was trying to be what everyone else wanted or expected me to be, but I didn't know what *I* wanted to be. This meant I ended up trying to take everything on. For a while I lost myself. I was pretty clear on my strengths and even the things that I wasn't so good at, but I was really unclear on the things that were most important to me and the type of leader I wanted to be.

Purpose

I am embarrassed when I think back on my early days as a people leader. I was a twenty-three-year-old female leading a group of seasoned sales professionals, and I took my cues from the few leaders I had known and from school teachers. I remember standing at the back of the room and shushing the team during meetings, which was probably not very helpful. As I progressed, I mellowed a bit, but I continued to try to take on board any and all feedback I received. This was back in the early nineties and for the most part that feedback involved me taking on more traditionally masculine leadership traits – I distinctly remember being told I needed to 'bang the table more'. The constant striving to be what I thought others wanted me to be was exhausting and confusing. As the mother of two small children, I clearly recall driving to work and feeling like I was putting on a different persona on the way, then relaxing back into who I really was as I drove home again at the end of the day. Some days I felt like I was being torn in two.

My naturally empathetic and empowering style certainly showed up, especially in my one-to-one interactions with people, and I am grateful for this. It helped to overshadow some of the imitative behaviours I was displaying in my attempts to be successful. I received positive feedback for these 'softer' types of behaviour, but because they came naturally to me, I thought they must not be right. I wasted a lot of time and missed opportunities by worrying about all the things I wasn't doing or being.

When I made the decision to step back and take the time to understand myself better by reflecting on what was important to me and how I wanted to lead, it freed me to focus on those things. Empathy and empowerment featured strongly in the list. The process wasn't easy. One of the things that helped me most was to think about my retirement and what I would like people to say about me at that point in my life. What was the legacy I wanted to leave? What would I want my family to say about me? What would I want my team members to say about me? What would I want my peers to say about me? What would I want my bosses to say about me? I forced myself to write my ideas and thought processes down. This reflective exercise helped me become clear on my drivers and this enabled me to start shaping a personal purpose statement.

Crafting the purpose statement was difficult – it was really tempting to put it off or to overthink it. In the end, I decided to do it partly by intuition. What I created resonated with me, although at the time I didn't think it would make a huge difference. It did. My purpose for many years now has been *'to bring my whole self to everything that I do and to create the conditions for others to do the same'.* I am driven in this by a deep belief that when we are able to bring our whole selves, we are able to unlock our potential, and that delivers exceptional results. From my own experience, hiding who we are in order to try and fit other people's expectations is just draining.

Leaning into my purpose and bringing it to life has been incredibly fulfilling both personally and professionally. Leading from a sense of purpose has focused me and given me energy. My purpose statement seemed like words on a page when I first wrote it down, but it has crafted and shaped the choices I have made, how I have interacted with others and the way I have led. When I retired recently after thirty years in the same organisation, I was gratified to hear this purpose reflected back to me in the farewell speeches others made. I have also had the privilege of seeing others thrive when they develop a clear sense of purpose for themselves and start leading authentically from that purpose.

Knowing yourself and developing your purpose starts with understanding what is really important to you. This becomes critical when thinking about balance. I believe you can have everything, but you can't have it all at once. If you don't know what is important to you, it is hard to set priorities and boundaries. Without boundaries and a lot of discipline, work will expand to fill every hour of every day, and then some. This can mean you miss out on spending time with the people you care about or doing the things that bring you joy and fulfilment. It can also lead to burnout. When you know what is important to you, you can be clear about the boundaries that are important to you and the things you never want to miss, and this will drive the choices you make.

We are often faced with difficult decisions. For example, you may be offered a promotion that requires you to move countries. You may be in a dual career relationship or have specific childcare needs. You may be torn. You are probably ambitious and want to get ahead... but at what cost? International experience can be exciting and hugely valuable but only if it works for your personal circumstances. Your experience abroad might bring you nothing but stress and sadness if it doesn't work for your life. I have coached many people struggling with this dilemma. When you are clear about what is most important to you it makes these decisions easier – not painless, but easier.

In 2015 I was working as a General Manager in Australia and juggling the needs of my adult son, who had severe depression and was living in New Zealand. It wasn't an ideal situation, but I could get to him relatively easily on a regular basis and was able for the most part to support his needs and manage the business requirements. I had long desired to become a Regional President and was offered the opportunity to move to Singapore to take up an Asia Pacific Leadership role. It was my dream job. I didn't have to think about it too long, however, to realise that it would not work for me to be further away from my son. Whilst I was ambitious and career-driven, in the end, it was a fairly easy decision to turn the role down. Even when I was offered the opportunity to do the role based in Australia, I knew I would not be able to fulfil the travel and other demands of the role in a way that would satisfy me and still be able to be there for my son.

It is worthwhile to reflect on and re-clarify your priorities and boundaries at least once a year as they can change depending on your personal circumstances. Most workplaces today will support your boundaries if you are clear and consistent about them. When I turned down the Regional President role, I never expected that I would be given the same opportunity again two years later, when my son was more settled. This time, I was able to accept.

Knowing ourselves helps us avoid the trap of blindly chasing 'success' without fully defining what we want that to look like for us. Without reflecting on what is important to you, it is easy to chase the outward symbols of success, without fully counting the cost.

Development and Growth

Your self-awareness is also critical to your personal development. As John C. Maxwell says, *"to grow yourself you must know yourself."* Understanding your strengths, your drivers, the things that you are not so good at and the things you really don't like, can help you find roles where you will flourish. When you know your strengths and the things you love to do and are in a role that leverages those things, you will thrive.

I have often sat in performance review discussions with my team members. I always start by sharing with them all the things I think they have been doing well. Invariably, when I begin to mention the one or two small areas they could improve on, all of a sudden, they pull out their pens and start to write. I have stopped them and said, "No – if you aren't going to write down all the things you are doing well, then don't write down the one or two things you could improve on." I think many of us fall into this trap. You desire to improve and be successful, so you focus intently on developing your weaknesses. I love Marcus Buckingham's books: *First Break All the Rules* and *Now, Discover Your Strengths*. Further building your strengths will always result in better outcomes than focusing on your weaker areas.

At the same time, I am not one of those who subscribes to the idea that you can't improve or shouldn't be aware of the things that may hold you back. On the contrary, I believe in learning constantly and working to be the best version of yourself. Being aware of the things you are not so good at is important, so you can seek help when you need it and avoid unnecessary pitfalls. As you get into leadership roles this allows you to bring people around you who are strong in the areas you are weak so that together you can succeed. But focusing solely on trying to strengthen a weakness can drain your energy and will not deliver the same benefits as building on the things you are already good at.

Being honest with yourself is not always easy. There are so many traps you can fall into, and 'imposter syndrome' can creep in. Negative self-talk sometimes seems to come much more freely than positive, encouraging self-talk. When you reflect on your own skills and behaviours, think about how you would talk to a good friend or a member of your team. Be honest with yourself about what you are doing well and where you need to improve and be at least as kind to yourself as you would be to them.

Knowing yourself also entails understanding the impact you have on others – being aware of how you show up in different situations. A good leader is able to read others' responses and adjust their own style accordingly. Leaders who are not strong in this area can miss important cues and blunder on, demotivating others and negatively impacting their results. In assessing potential, I have often been in conversations with other senior leaders about people who display obvious potential but lack self-awareness, and this is holding them back.

This type of self-knowledge requires more than self-reflection although that is an important place to start. You also need to check in with a range of people in different situations to understand how you are being perceived. This could be as simple as being tuned into the body language in a room, but cultivating trusting relationships where you can be given good, actionable feedback is also extremely helpful. More on cultivating feedback in Chapter Four.

Where to start:

Some people find self-reflection relatively easy. Others need to reflect over a longer period of time to allow things to come to the surface. Regardless of your preference, I encourage you to make time and create a space free of interruptions, ideally a space where you feel comfortable and inspired. Some people like to use visuals to help; others like to have music playing. Choose a time, place and context that will best help you to delve below the surface and discover what makes you tick. Make notes as you go but resist the urge to leap to the outcome before you have given yourself time to reflect.

Start by considering the following questions:

- What am I really good at? (Think about feedback, performance reviews, etc.)
- What gives me energy? (Activities, people, environments)
- What things do I struggle with or am I less skilled at?
- What drains my energy? (Activities, people, environments)
- What are my primary values? Think about the things you would really make a stand for. If someone crosses a value for you it will generally result in a very strong, often defensive reaction.
- What do you want to be remembered for? (By the people who matter to you most? By your work colleagues?)
- What boundaries do you want to set between your personal and work life? Are there important occasions you never want to miss? Do you have childcare or elder parent care responsibilities? How are you maintaining your health and physical fitness?
- Where do you get support when things are challenging? This one is important to understand – too often we neglect our own support network and when things get difficult, we don't know where to turn.
- Where are you today and where do you want to be in five... ten... twenty years? Think about this in terms of a holistic life: career, family, friends, finances, spirituality, hobbies.

Once you have reflected on these questions and feel comfortable with your responses, the next step is to pull it all together:

- What does this tell you about what is most important to you?
- How does this inform your purpose?
- How does this resonate across both your personal and professional life?
- Begin to craft a purpose statement – something that will guide you and help you make choices and decisions for the long term.
- What are you already doing that supports your purpose?
- What things do you need to stop, change or add to be able to live your purpose more consistently?

Your purpose statement doesn't have to be carefully crafted or 'word-smithed' to perfection. It just needs to be meaningful to you. Whether you ever share it with anyone else or not is your own decision. It is intended to guide your choices and priorities so make sure it works for you.

Sometimes self-reflection leads you to realise you are in the wrong job or need to make some other changes on your path. It can be scary. Knowing what is important to you, and how others think and feel about you and your behaviour, is also how you get started on a path to greater fulfilment. Ultimately, that will lead you to greater success.

As you reflect, it is vital to distinguish between what is important to you and what you think other people want or expect – and to focus on the former. This can be very difficult, especially if it puts you in conflict with people you care about. I remember coaching a young woman through this process. She was struggling with entrenched family expectations that she would be a stay-at-home mum, while she felt that society expected her to be out working. She had been very successful in her career to date and was identified as a future potential talent in the company where she worked. It took her some time to figure out what *she* wanted for herself, and she was then able to shape a successful and fulfilling career while remaining a loving, caring and available mother.

Once you have answered these questions and defined your purpose, you are on the path to knowing yourself better.

Knowing yourself is a lifelong journey, not a 'once and done' exercise. New experiences, new relationships and outside events will all continue to shape who you are. For that reason, I recommend reviewing these questions at least once a year. For me, this became a bit of a ritual during year-end vacations, when I was not so distracted by the demands of daily life and had the time and space to reconsider my priorities and drivers. You will need to find what works for you.

Nelson Mandela expressed this very well when he said, "Learn to know yourself... to search regularly the processes of your own mind and feelings." Knowing yourself and what is important to you is a fundamental step to unleashing your fullest potential.

CHAPTER TWO
VULNERABILITY

"Vulnerability is the birthplace of innovation, creativity and change."

– Brene Brown

"Vulnerability sounds like truth and feels like courage. Truth and courage aren't always comfortable, but they're never weakness."

– Brene Brown

You may have the perception that leaders have it all together: this can be far from the reality. All leaders are human beings, with their own fears and foibles. A vulnerable leader is more accessible and therefore builds trust more readily. They create the space for learning and growing – for themselves and for those around them.

In my interpretation, vulnerability is having the courage to be open with others about what is true for me. This means sharing, with wisdom, what is happening for me. It means talking about my fears and failures as well as what is working. Vulnerability is also about being open and responsive to feedback, being willing to learn, and trying new things.

It is worth expending a few sentences on what vulnerability is not. It is not about sharing videos to social media of you crying in the car, nor is it describing every intimate detail of your personal life. Over-sharing can have a negative impact. Vulnerability is about being real about who you are and what is important to you, being open to feedback and admitting mistakes. Ultimately, it is a critical enabler to learning and growing.

I opened this chapter with two quotes from Brene Brown. She is, in my opinion, the leading expert on vulnerability and I highly recommend her book *Daring Greatly*. It resonates extremely well with my own experience and helped me to keep going when I sometimes questioned whether being vulnerable was really the right approach. She has written many books on this subject and I am trying to tackle it in a chapter. I am just scraping the surface.

My first lesson in vulnerability at work came quite early in my career. I was struggling to trust my boss, and many of my teammates felt the same way. It is not easy to be at your best when trust is absent. I don't remember exactly how it happened, but I do remember being in a one-to-one conversation with my boss. I distinctly recall the feeling of dread as the emotion welled within me, and I practically blurted out that I was struggling with trusting him. I hadn't planned to share this with him, so I hadn't prepared what to say. In the moment it just felt right.

It felt incredibly scary, and yet I realised almost the second the words left my mouth that by voicing what I felt, the power of that feeling diminished.

Looking back on that moment, it was also a very clear lesson that vulnerability means speaking up when you have absolutely no control over how anyone else will respond. That is what makes it feel so scary. My speaking up led to a conversation about where my concerns were coming from, and this moved our working relationship to a very different level. The act of speaking about my lack of trust inherently built a significant amount of trust.

You may be thinking, "I could never do that; you don't know my boss," or something similar. And certainly, every situation is different. However, my experience has always been that opening up and being honest about what I feel, my concerns, fears and hopes has always helped my relationships to move forward. This doesn't mean being blunt, rude or insubordinate. Thinking about the language you use, your tone of voice, and the timing and location of the conversation are important.

The critical thing about vulnerability is owning your emotions for yourself and not blaming or judging the emotions of others. I did not tell my boss he was untrustworthy or was doing anything to break trust. I just explained that I was struggling to trust him. The conversation was about me and what I needed to do to be able to move the relationship forward. After years of practising this, I am now much more afraid of the impact of not having this type of conversation than I am of the perceived ramifications of being vulnerable – those stories we tell ourselves that stop us from speaking up. Allowing unspoken stories to develop and build can severely limit us from being our best and most effective.

Why is this important? Relationships are a key factor in our lives. A relationship built on half-truths, unspoken or hidden factors takes a huge amount of energy and is significantly less fulfilling than a relationship built on trust and openness. In any relationship, you can only be responsible for your contribution. How the other party or parties respond is up to them. Sharing your own fears, weaknesses and concerns in a constructive way is an invitation for others to do the same, opening the relationship to become deeper, more meaningful and more fulfilling.

You may think this all sounds fine – but for your personal relationships, not at work. I argue that we spend a huge amount of our time at work and are almost always dependent on others to help deliver the results we strive for. Building strong, trusting and enduring working relationships creates an engaging and positive environment that helps drive consistent results. These strong foundations become even more critical when things get tough.

Being vulnerable can feel extremely scary. It takes courage to share what is going on for you, but the rewards of that courage are real. Think about a time when you watched someone giving a speech or making a presentation. It was obvious they were nervous, and they said something like, "I'm sorry, I'm really nervous." You probably immediately felt empathy and wanted to support them to succeed. By speaking out what they were feeling, they reduced the power of that feeling and even enrolled the audience as their supporters. It may not have taken all their nerves away, but it certainly helped to settle them and engage the audience. This is the hidden power of vulnerability.

Wisdom: The Partner of Vulnerability

The partner of vulnerability is wisdom: knowing what to share, when to share, who to share with, and how much to share. Blurting out your biggest weaknesses, greatest failures and most embarrassing moments at your first meeting is probably not wisdom. But equally, hiding all your faults, acting like you know everything and can do it all, can have its own downside. At its worst, it could make you appear aloof, defensive or out of touch, and this can lead to distrust.

Over-sharing in the workplace is not wisdom. No one needs to know all the intimate details of your personal life. But equally, battling through a significant personal issue and not telling anyone at work about it can be problematic. Even the best of us struggle to be on top form at work when we are facing upheaval in our personal lives. Sharing what is going on, confidentially, with your boss, a trusted peer, Human Resources or a teammate, can enable the business to provide extra support or flexibility when you need it.

When my son was at the deepest point in his depression, it was very difficult for me. I was responsible for a large business and many people depended on me for leadership. And my son needed me too. My concern for him took up a lot of my emotional and mental energy. I shared selectively with a few key team members, my boss and Human Resources. Knowing that a few people at work understood at least a bit of what I was dealing with was hugely helpful. It gave me the space I needed to be there emotionally, and at times physically, for my son, knowing others would cover for me at work if I needed them to. This also motivated me to bring my best to the business whenever I was able.

There is also wisdom in telling people what you are focusing on to become even better at what you do. Sharing the results of the 360-degree feedback that I referenced in the introduction chapter felt incredibly scary at the time. I was so devastated by the impact I was having that at first, I was embarrassed to share. In hindsight, I understand that by sharing my feedback and making a commitment to improve, my team and those around me became invested in supporting me. They became my greatest source of feedback, guidance and help to get back on course. They also became my biggest cheerleaders, encouraging me to keep at it and letting me know when the changes I was attempting to make were working.

I contrast this with an earlier time. I was the General Manager of the New Zealand business, and had just returned from a week-long development program in the US. I decided to try out some new behaviours in response to some feedback I had received on the program. I had been told that I was doing too much for the team and not giving them enough space to work things out for themselves.

At our next team meeting, I made a conscious, but unspoken, decision to sit back and let the team sort things out for themselves. About forty-five minutes into the meeting, I had barely said a word. The conversation was going in circles, I was frustrated, and the rest of the team were completely confused. Finally, one of them asked me what was wrong. When I explained what I was trying to do they all heaved a sigh of relief. Because I hadn't explained that I was going to be trying out some new behaviours and told them why, they had all made up their own stories about why I was behaving differently. And their stories all had some sinister motive to them – another very valuable lesson.

Things started to go a lot more smoothly straight away and the team were happy to step up and embrace more responsibility. It is important to remember that people are not mind readers.

People often put leaders on some sort of pedestal, assuming that they have everything together or are somehow 'super-human'. This can make leaders seem unapproachable and achieving a senior leadership position seem unattainable. I have even seen this result in people 'opting out' of aspiring to leadership positions. The reality is that even the most senior leaders still put their pants on one leg at a time. They have their own foibles; they all make mistakes and have all had their own 'oh shit' moments.

I have participated in discussion forums as part of development programs for upcoming leaders where other senior leaders and I shared our crucible moments, the stories of our worst times. These sessions are often called out by the participants as one of the highlights of the program, primarily because they help to show the human side of leaders and help the participants realise that they are not alone in their vulnerabilities and the challenges they face.

Vulnerability and Development

Vulnerability starts with being honest with yourself. Listen to what is going on inside you. Acknowledge the things you are struggling with. Recognise that no one is perfect, including you. Vulnerability is an excellent way to overcome defensiveness. If it is okay not to be perfect, then receiving feedback from others or acknowledging an area of weakness suddenly feels less scary. This creates the space for learning and development to occur.

By contrast, if you are not open to admitting when something has gone wrong or that you need help, it is hard to improve, and you may end up stuck. Vulnerability is also a huge help in supporting the development of others. By role modelling openness and the willingness to learn and grow, you create an environment where it is safe for others to do the same. This is at the heart of unleashing potential.

There is an abundance of research linking psychological safety with innovation. Even when I think I have the right answer, I could be wrong. Being vulnerable has helped me to create an environment where it is okay for others to challenge me and for different points of view to be heard. This leads to better creativity and problem solving, often resulting in a much better outcome. Role modelling this level of openness and supporting others when they respond with their own vulnerability creates a psychologically safe environment.

Different cultures have different expectations around sharing and openness. When I first started working in Asia people told me that vulnerability wouldn't work. I was told, "It is much more hierarchical here and people won't respect you if you show vulnerability. People here like to see strong leaders who have all the answers."

But not showing vulnerability would have been inauthentic for me. I was gentle. I cultivated relationships and sought regular feedback. And my experience has been that vulnerability works just as well in Asian cultures as in western ones. In fact, having worked with people in over fifty countries, I have not had a negative response anywhere. I have learned a huge amount from being open and candid and I have seen others learn and grow too. I firmly believe that vulnerability appeals to all humans, regardless of cultural expectations.

Practising Vulnerability

There are lots of ways to start practising vulnerability. Here are a few suggestions to get you started. The more you practise it the easier it will get.

Share your development plan with a trusted peer. Seek their feedback and support.

Talk to your team and let them know you want to start being more open with them to create an environment that will foster learning and growth. Ask them what questions they have for you and be as honest as you can with the answers.

Practice using 'I' statements to express yourself. This is a way to take ownership of your reactions and feelings. Avoid blaming others. For example, say, "I feel sad/cross/frustrated when ...." rather than, 'You make me feel sad/cross/frustrated when ...".

Get into the habit of listening to what is going on for you. When you start to feel uncomfortable it may be a sign that there is something you need to express. Even saying you feel uncomfortable can be a good start to open up a useful exploratory conversation.

"Authenticity is a collection of choices that we have to make every day. It's about the choice to show up and be real. The choice to be honest. The choice to let our true selves be seen."

– Brene Brown

It is almost impossible to be authentic without being vulnerable. Allowing others to see who you are and what is important to you opens the path for deeper relationships to develop. Deeper relationships encourage trust, and trust creates a positive environment that encourages learning and growth. These are the conditions that help people to be at their best, and to deliver outstanding results.

CHAPTER THREE
LISTENING

"One of the most sincere forms of respect is actually listening to what another has to say."

– Bryan H. McGill

I am convinced that listening is one of, if not the, most under-rated leadership competency. Real listening opens our minds to better understand others' perspectives and points of view. It enables empathy and leads to better, more informed decision making. Good listening is critical to conflict management. All it requires is a bit of patience and the willingness to suspend your own views long enough to hear someone else's.

Despite this, very little time is spent teaching people how to listen effectively, and listening rarely shows up on the development plan of senior leaders. I believe this is a huge miss as listening, deeply and with real intent, is the foundation for so many other competencies. I have met many people who claim to be good listeners, but who are, in reality, only listening to what they want to hear, while they prepare what they want to say.

When I was a child there was a poster on the wall of the bedroom I shared with my sister. It read:

> *"A wise old bird sat on the oak;*
> *the more he saw the less he spoke;*
> *the less he spoke, the more he heard;*
> *why can't we be like that wise old bird?"*

I have no idea where the rhyme came from, but I have always remembered it, even if, at the time, I didn't fully understand the wisdom it contained.

Think about a time when you felt really heard and understood. What was the context and how did the person demonstrate their listening? How did being heard help deliver a better outcome? Now think about a time when you were not listened to. What was the impact on you, on your relationships and on the results you were trying to achieve? Which impact would you rather have on the people you work with?

Listening Unlocks Debate

Have you ever sat in a room and listened to two people engaged in an animated discussion? Both people passionately argue their case, without hearing each other. When listening dispassionately you can often find the commonality between the two and help to mediate. I have even seen people passionately agreeing with each other, but because they aren't listening, they keep arguing their point.

This common, learned method of driving forward rarely results in a positive outcome. A deadlock often remains. Other times the person who is the most stubborn or the most senior 'wins' the argument, even if it does not result in the best outcome. Sometimes this sort of behaviour results in circular discussions that carry on for months. Even when apparent agreement has been reached, if one party doesn't feel heard it is unlikely they will fully support the 'agreed' direction. Instead of all parties committing to what was 'agreed' it can result in those who didn't feel heard becoming passively resistant or even actively undermining the decision.

By contrast, when two people step back, dispassionately examine an issue and listen intently to each other, they are usually able to find effective solutions that everyone can get behind and support. At the end of the day, a 'bad' decision that is fully supported is far more likely to deliver positive results than a good decision that is not fully supported. This may sound counterintuitive but as John Doerr says, *"Ideas are easy; execution is everything."*

I am certainly not suggesting going with a bad idea just to avoid a disagreement. However, I have seen hours, days, weeks, months and years of wasted effort, trying to implement good decisions that are not supported because people haven't felt heard. In these situations nothing gets achieved. Going with an alternative option that people will support and buy into will get you much further.

At its heart, the art of listening is simple. It means leaving behind your own opinions, at least long enough to fully hear the opinions of others. Even if, after listening intently and gaining a clear understanding of another's opinion, you remain convinced that your opinion is better, you will have identified areas of common ground or intent. This makes it much easier to pitch your own viewpoint in a way that addresses the concerns and hopes of the other party. Essentially, if you want to influence others, you need to be open to being influenced by them. When everyone leaves their own views to one side, listens to each other and focuses on finding the best overall outcome, you are able to deliver collective success.

You may be thinking that this only works when both people are listening. That certainly helps, but it is not critical. Even when only one party listens intently, with a genuine desire to understand all other parties' views, their ability to influence increases. This is because two things happen when you truly listen to someone. Firstly, they feel respected, heard and valued, and are therefore much more likely to consider alternatives. Secondly, the better you understand the rationale behind someone's argument, the better you are able to frame a different viewpoint in a way that it may be heard, and the more likely you are to be able to reach an effective compromise.

You may even find that when you listen with genuine intent to understand, you change your view altogether. I can think of many times when I started with a clear view on the direction I wanted the team to take. After listening to different viewpoints we collectively made a different decision. Whether this was the right decision or not, because people felt heard and understood, the team aligned and we delivered great results. If I had pushed ahead blindly with my own ideas without hearing the views of others, I expect we would have experienced a lot more conflict and less positive outcomes.

A Word About Active Listening

You may have been trained in 'active listening'. In principle, the concepts behind active listening are excellent. Too often, though, I have seen people come away from Active Listening training without a real change in their approach. They may have learned to become good at mirroring or repeating what the other person has said. Unfortunately, they have neglected to go beyond the surface to really understand the other person's views. This on its own is not active listening.

By definition, active listening is active. It involves a mindset shift, to move from thinking about your points of view and what you want to say, to being genuinely curious about what the other person is saying. Active listening requires active questioning. Seek to go beyond what the person is saying to understand what they are not saying. Too often we make up our own stories and assumptions to fill in the blanks. Oftentimes we get it very wrong. Asking good questions about what has not been said can help avoid this. Any time invested in listening will be well rewarded.

Knowing Others

In Chapter One, we discussed knowing yourself. Equally important is to know the people you have relationships with, whether those are personal or professional relationships. Knowing someone else only happens when you listen to them.

I have always been interested in understanding the people I work with. Knowing their interests, their ambitions, and as much as they are willing to share about their personal situations helps me understand how to support them to be their best. And this became even more apparent to me during the pandemic when we were all in lockdown.

I was a Regional President at the time, responsible for businesses throughout Asia Pacific and Russia. I was used to travelling extensively and meeting with the teams in person on a regular basis. Obviously, this was no longer possible. Asia was a bit ahead of the curve in terms of the timing of the pandemic. Many of the countries in my region, including China, were locking down, while those in Europe (where my head office was located) were still only just starting to be impacted. In contrast, by the time Europe was fully in lockdown many of the Asian countries were starting to open up again, and this see-saw continued for months.

I made a conscious decision to be intentional about meeting each person I dealt with 'where they were at'. Every conversation I had started with an open discussion about how the person was and what was happening for them. I remember several calls with some of my senior team during which we spent our entire time allocation discussing how they felt and the challenges they were facing at home. Others were opportunities for people to express frustration at the corporate communications that focused on what was happening in Europe and didn't reflect the situation in their own country. Some people just wanted to focus on the business and how to keep things moving forward. I applied this listening approach with my peers and superiors, and in fact with everyone I connected with.

Giving people this time and space in the conversation may have appeared indulgent, or even irresponsible, particularly given the crisis conditions the pandemic was creating for us all. On the contrary, by meeting my team members and colleagues where they were at, I was able to provide the support they needed so that they could do the same for others. Collectively we were stronger and better equipped because of these conversations. Having dealt with numerous crises over the years, I am convinced that it is even more important during a crisis to make the time to connect with people in a meaningful way.

I had never really thought about this approach to listening as anything unique. One week, in the middle of the pandemic, I was struggling myself. My daughter and her boyfriend had travelled to Europe on their big OE (overseas experience) before the pandemic broke out. They were living in a van over there and trying to figure out a way to get home. They were extremely stressed, and we were spending long hours on the phone trying to figure things out.

At the same time, my son was involved in a very serious bike accident back in New Zealand. I was working in Singapore and was unable to get back to New Zealand because of quarantine requirements. I was also juggling the demands of the business. I remember getting to the end of a week of conversations with different people across the business, doing lots of my usual listening and asking lots of questions about how everyone was doing. I realised that not once during that time had anyone asked me how I was. I felt very alone.

I have fantastic colleagues, and I am sure that if I had volunteered what was happening for me to any of them, I would have received great support. I recognised that when I was struggling, I was much less likely to volunteer the information. If someone had asked how I was, I would certainly have shared. I believe this is true for many of us and this realisation stood as an important and valuable lesson.

Listening to what is not said is as important as listening to what is said. This includes noting body language, as well as subjects that are avoided, for example, noticing the person or people who have been quiet during a meeting and inviting them to share their opinion. This doesn't mean forcing them to have an opinion, merely inviting them by asking what they think. I have often seen reflective thinkers make extremely valuable contributions to a conversation when they are invited this way. It would have been a shame to miss their input.

In fact, reflective thinkers often leave meetings feeling frustrated that no one noticed they had something to add. The quicker thinkers/louder talkers may not leave space for other views. Noticing someone's reactions or body language can help people feel valued and open up some great insights. I do this by framing it as a question: "I noticed that your expression changed then – what was that about?" or: "You looked like you might have wanted to say something then?" It is important not to force a response – I try to be as self-effacing as possible when I make these comments: "It could just be my imagination but ..." works quite well too. Making deliberate efforts to make eye contact with all participants and to notice everyone's body language will maximise input and help all participants feel valued.

I should point out here that I am by no means perfect at the art of listening. My daughter regularly points out when I am not giving her my full attention. And I can get as distracted as anyone. But I make it a priority when I am in a conversation with someone to give them my undivided attention. I don't take my phone into meetings. I keep my computer closed or switched off. Equally, I let people know if I don't have time to give them my attention right now, and instead arrange a time to connect when I will be able to focus on them. Making this a priority has helped me build stronger relationships with my team and my colleagues. The relationships that develop when real active listening is practised lead to better leadership, greater teamwork, and better results.

The Importance of One-to-One Time

It is worth stressing the value of committing to one-to-one sessions on a regular basis with your direct reports. Depending on their level of seniority and experience, this could be on a daily, weekly or monthly basis. Even when I had in excess of twenty direct reports, I made it an absolute priority to connect with each of them once every four weeks. This time was scheduled into our calendars well in advance. My team regularly expressed to me how helpful they found this time.

These sessions are important for getting to know your team members, to understand their needs, hopes and concerns and to support their development. Ideally, this time becomes your team member's time to get their needs met. The following simple structure is a guide to make these sessions helpful. It can be easily modified based on the responses and needs of each individual. I generally allocated forty-five minutes for each session – some people took a little longer, others a little less time.

- Start by asking how they are. Listen carefully and probe to understand what is going on for them, personally and at work. Give this as much time as it needs and avoid the temptation to rush straight to business matters.
- Check in on work priorities. What are they focused on right now? What help or assistance do they need?
- Is there anything happening with their team that you need to be aware of or that they need support with?
- Check in on development and learning. How are they progressing with their career and self-development goals? What else might they need support with?
- Lastly, are there any non-urgent work matters that have come up since your last connection that you need to share with them?

'Listening' as the Basis for Communication

This might be a bit of a stretch for a chapter on listening but if you think about listening as understanding the person/people you are engaging with, it can form a solid basis for all communication. One of the mistakes I have seen many people make is trying to communicate the same message exactly the same way to different audiences. Taking a few minutes to step back and reflect on what is really important to your audience will help you frame your messages in ways such that they can be better received.

I used to make the mistake of underestimating how much senior leaders understood about my business. I had a tendency to over-communicate, particularly around the details. Senior leaders are busy and tend to have shorter attention spans. When I thought about what they really needed to know I became much better at developing shorter, story-style presentations and found that this created more positive results.

Take a moment to think about your audience any time you are about to share information. 'Listen' to what is important to them and use this to frame the message you share. I have learned over the years that less is generally more. People can always ask questions if they want more detail.

Listening Can Be Uncomfortable

There are many ways to demonstrate listening. Asking great, open-ended questions and following up with further relevant questions to go deeper, demonstrates genuine interest. Simple requests like *tell me more*, also open the conversation to a deeper level, especially when accompanied by receptive body language and eye contact. Silence is also powerful as it leaves space for the other person to go deeper. When you listen with genuine intent, you build a level of trust in a relationship that can lead to people sharing information that may make you feel uncomfortable.

When someone shares about a relationship issue, a problem child, a family member with ill health, or a mental health challenge, it can be extremely uncomfortable. Many times, you may want to offer some sympathy and end the conversation as quickly as possible. Staying in that space, and sitting with that discomfort, is extremely powerful.

It is important when someone shares this type of information to realise that they are not looking to you for answers.

Unless you are a qualified professional, even trying to offer solutions would be inappropriate. What they are looking for is genuine empathy, someone to listen and just be there for them. Silence can be useful. Acknowledging their pain and offering your time as a listening ear will build trust like nothing else.

Everyone has a story. We all struggle with different things at different times. When someone has trusted you with such a deep and personal disclosure, one of the greatest ways to show respect is by giving them the space to share what they are experiencing, without judgement and without advice. It may be appropriate to encourage them to seek professional support. If your business offers an Employee Assistance Program or similar this can provide a great option. The most important thing, though, is not to rush through and move on. I find it helpful to ask what they would like from me, and it stops me from leaping to my own conclusions.

Tips for Great Listening

Great listening starts with an open mindset and a genuine intention to seek to understand. It demands curiosity and a little patience.

- Give people your full attention. Shut down other distractions and if possible, go somewhere quiet where you will not be interrupted. If you don't have the time now, tell them, and make a commitment to connect when you do have the time. Make time with others a priority and schedule it like you would any other business matter.

- Practise asking open-ended questions. Follow up with more questions to gain greater understanding – don't just skim across the surface. Some great conversation openers are things like:
  - o What's going on for you?
  - o Tell me more about that.
  - o How did you feel about that?
  - o What concerns do you have about...?
  - o What excites you about...?
  - o What support do you need?

- Be aware of listening bias. It is common to listen for information that supports your view and to miss things that might suggest a different opinion. Actively seeking divergent views will lead to a more robust outcome and is a good way to avoid bias. This is particularly important when making big decisions that carry significant risk.

- Catch yourself when you start formulating your responses before the other person has finished speaking. Try and stay focused on fully understanding their point of view.
- Practise silence with empathy. When I was working in Human Resources many years ago, I used to focus on nodding and smiling gently. It is simple but effective in many situations.

I love this quote from L J Isham. To me, it really sums up what listening is about. *"Listening is an attitude of the heart, a genuine desire to be with another, which both attracts and heals."*

CHAPTER FOUR
FEEDBACK

"Feedback is the breakfast of champions."

– Ken Blanchard

Good, honest, timely feedback, delivered in an effective way, is one of the greatest gifts you can give or receive. Feedback is a critical element in growth: your growth, and the growth of the people you work with and lead. Without feedback, you will only see things through your own lens, and you risk missing important information about how you are perceived, and how you can be better.

I believe strongly in the mantra that feedback is a gift. It doesn't matter if that feedback is positive, encouraging you to do more of the same, or if that feedback is corrective, helping you to understand what is not working so well. Receiving feedback with grace and curiosity, and with a positive intention to understand others' views will help you to hone your ability to lead effectively.

Even more importantly, it role models to others the benefits of feedback and helps them to seek, accept, and act on the feedback of others. You cannot reasonably expect your team members to receive feedback in a positive and constructive manner if you constantly deflect or defend against any feedback you receive. I am sure you have seen great examples of leaders receiving and acting on feedback, and probably also great examples of the opposite.

Impact and Intent

In general, we have a tendency to judge ourselves by our intent, and to judge others by their impact. This makes sense. Without good communication, only you know the intent behind your words and actions. You know exactly what you mean and how you intend for that to sound. The actual impact on the other person may be very different. Both are subjective, based on what each of you knows and experiences, and therefore both are valid. This is why objective feedback and active listening are so important. When you deliver feedback with empathy, in a way that can be heard and understood, it builds trust and supports growth.

Without effective communication you only experience the impact of others' words and actions. This often results in leaps of judgement as you create your own story about the other's intent. When the impact is not positive, the tendency is to create a story of negative intent, rather than assuming positive intent. I have often heard the mantra 'assume positive intent' but I have rarely seen it well implemented. The only real way to close the gap between intent and impact is to have a conversation, because our assumptions are often wrong.

This is one of the most critical learnings I took from the feedback I referred to in the introduction chapter. I had completed a survey about the impact I wanted to have in the organisation (my intent) and received 360-degree feedback showing the actual impact I was having. I was devastated by the feedback showing a significant gap between my intent and my impact. I processed the feedback with my coach, and I vividly recall a conversation I had with him. After about thirty minutes of discussion one day, he stopped me and said, "Do you realise you have told me about fifty times in the last half hour how frustrated you are?"

He went on to explain that frustration is one of the most negative emotions we can experience, second only to guilt. He also explained that frustration generally comes from our expectations not being met. He encouraged me to reflect. Either I was not making my expectations clear, or I was expecting someone who always did things one way, to magically change and do them another way. This was leading to me being frustrated. And that frustration was having an extremely negative impact on the way others were experiencing me, regardless of my positive intentions for the way I wanted to lead.

This stopped me in my tracks. I suddenly understood much more about what had been happening. I remembered a recent meeting I had led. There were several people sitting around the table. The sales team were explaining the recent shortfall in their results. Inside, I was fuming because it seemed to me that they were making excuses rather than taking accountability and looking for potential solutions.

I took a deep breath and tried to calm myself (positive intent). What I didn't realise was that my body language and tone of voice were broadcasting my frustration very clearly to the whole room. I kept my voice quiet and said something like, "Thank you for that explanation; in future it would be great if you could propose some potential solutions rather than just explaining what is not working."

I was surprised at the reactions in the room. People looked stressed and concerned. I had been pleased with myself for not losing my temper, but the dejected way people left the room suggested they weren't positively engaged.

Only later, after receiving the coaching I referred to above, and modifying the way I responded, did someone tell me that it had been one of the scariest meetings they had ever attended. My body language was so 'loud', the people around the table had no idea what was going to come out of my mouth. They developed their own interpretation of my body language, which was the opposite of my actual intent. Looking back now I can laugh at how easy it is to be misunderstood but this still resonates as one of my most powerful leadership learnings.

I realised that I was leaping to judgement based on my reactions to others' words and behaviour, rather than seeking to understand better their intentions. I thought they were making excuses and trying to avoid accountability. After checking in to better understand, I discovered that, in fact, they were taking so much accountability they were beating themselves up, and this was contributing to the way they were acting.

I was oblivious to the impact my body language and tone of voice were having on others. I set a new intention for myself: to judge myself by my impact and others by their intent. This required communication. I became laser focused on understanding my impact and sought feedback regularly from those around me. And I focused on working to understand others' intentions rather than judging their impact.

I set myself the mantra: "Perceiving before Judgement." I used to write this in large letters on a piece of paper and have it in front of me during meetings. It was a reminder to check in, especially when I started to feel that tell-tale reaction in my gut that I was getting frustrated. It prompted me to step back, take a breath and seek to understand what was going on rather than leaping to judgement.

At first, this took a lot of mental focus and practice. And I made a lot of mistakes. But because I had explained to my team what I was working on, they were very supportive and gave me valuable feedback when I got things right, and clear, actionable feedback when my impact was not positive. This helped me to continually adjust my responses. Over time I experienced frustration much less often. I learned that when I started to feel any frustration, I needed to take a minute to pause, and only respond when I was 'in neutral'. For me, this meant recognising a tightness in my gut, quickly identifying it as frustration and calming myself before making any response.

A very simple example of this was one evening when I was driving to the gym. I had a personal training appointment, and as usual, I had left it to the last minute to leave work. I was running a little late and the traffic light turned red. There was only one car in front of me. When the traffic light turned green, it took them a long time to move, and I missed the light. I felt that tightness of frustration. The old me would have fumed and made up a story about the incompetence of the other driver, but I caught myself.

I am sure the person driving the other car hadn't held me up on purpose. In fact, if I had left on time, it wouldn't have been a problem. I took responsibility for my own actions rather than blaming someone else for making me late. I immediately calmed down and was able to continue to the gym in a positive frame of mind. In this example, I didn't need to check in with the other person for feedback, but I share it to explain the process.

Cultivating and Receiving Feedback

I am focusing first on receiving feedback. If you want to give others feedback to support their development and growth, it is important that you role model receptivity to feedback yourself. If you want to be the best version of yourself that is possible, it is critical you understand the impact you are having and how it matches your intent.

Cultivating feedback starts with vulnerability. Let people know what you are working on and request feedback on specific behaviours. This can help people to feel more comfortable giving feedback and is often more useful than asking for general feedback. While it is good to encourage everyone to give you feedback, in addition, seek out people who you know will be prepared to tell you the truth and specifically ask them to observe and provide feedback on your behaviour. Ask your team, peers and others whom you trust to let you know if they see you making changes that work so you can continue to reinforce them. Ask them to let you know if you do things that have a negative impact. Ask them to be as specific as possible and to share examples.

However, asking explicitly for feedback is not enough. It can be daunting to give feedback to someone, especially if they are more senior than you. How you respond to feedback in the moment will make a big difference to how much feedback you receive. If you are defensive, and particularly if your mode of defence is to attack, you should not expect to receive feedback, and you will miss out on the valuable information you would otherwise receive. Even receiving positive feedback can be uncomfortable. If you consistently dismiss positive feedback, you will be unlikely to receive more and could be perceived by some as having false humility.

Remember that feedback is about the impact you had on someone else – how you were perceived by them. If they think it is important enough to mention, then take the time to listen and appreciate them. When receiving positive feedback, a simple thank you is often enough. If you are unclear on the feedback, asking questions for clarification is useful. Avoid dismissing or minimising the feedback for yourself. It can be tempting to minimise positive feedback by shrugging it off or ascribing it to someone else. Take a moment to reflect, acknowledge and appreciate that someone took the time to recognise you.

When receiving feedback that is more challenging, try and adopt a neutral expression. Thank the person for taking the time to give you the feedback and for being bold enough to do so. Acknowledge that you have heard what they have to say. Ask questions for clarification if necessary. It is very important that you do not justify or defend as this is likely to stop someone from giving you feedback in the future. Ask what behaviour they would have preferred to have seen in the situation. While examples can be helpful, avoid demanding proof of what they say. I have often seen this used as a form of defence. It can be tempting to dive into the specifics and use them to deflect or avoid the feedback. Let the person know you will reflect on their feedback and take it into account.

One of the best ways to show that you are genuine about receiving feedback is to act on the feedback you receive. Stephen Covey sums this up well: *"It takes humility to seek feedback. It takes wisdom to understand it, analyse it and appropriately act on it."*

This does not mean you have to act on every single piece of feedback you receive. You will not be able to please everyone all the time. Knowing yourself and understanding what is important to you becomes crucial when acting on feedback. For changes to be sustainable they need to be congruent with your values and goals. Acting on feedback is not about trying to be what someone else wants you to be. If you try to do this, you are likely to end up making lots of little, sometimes contradictory, changes. This will be confusing to the people around you and they are likely to question your authenticity. But if you never act on feedback, people will soon give up trying.

Remember that your goal is to be the best version of yourself. How you impact others is an important part of that. Feedback builds awareness of the impact you are having. Reflect on what you can do to either maintain a positive impact or what you can do to improve your positive impact, based on the feedback you received.

Once you have reflected on the feedback you have received and decided you want to try and adjust your behaviour, this can be a good opportunity to go back to the person who gave you the feedback and let them know. Ask them to observe and to let you know whether the changes you are making are having the desired impact. Also ask them to let you know if you are slipping into old habits, because change is not easy to maintain. Doing this engages their support and they are much more likely to give you helpful feedback *and* to support your positive intent.

Giving Effective Feedback

When we think about giving feedback we tend to think about negative or corrective feedback. In fact, positive feedback is equally important. Positive feedback helps people to feel valued, motivated and engaged. It reinforces and encourages positive behaviour. Providing regular positive feedback also helps people to hear and respond to corrective feedback in a constructive way. Actively look for things that are having a positive impact and make a habit of recognising them with feedback. This sounds simple but is often overlooked.

As mentioned earlier in the chapter, feedback is a gift. As a leader, providing regular, clear, actionable feedback is one of the best things you can do to support the development of your team. Numerous books have been written about giving feedback. I like to keep it as simple as possible. Regardless of whether the feedback is positive or corrective, following a few guidelines can help the feedback land well:

- Make the feedback as timely as possible. Don't dredge up issues from months ago. If the behaviour is important enough to address (either for positive recognition or for correction) do so as soon as possible after you see the behaviour.
- Unless you have specific permission to give feedback in public, find a quiet place where you will not be disturbed. Some people are uncomfortable even receiving praise in public.
- Be specific. Describe the situation, the behaviour you observed and the impact it had. Avoid the tendency to judge intention and, instead, focus on the impact.
- Own the feedback – this is the impact it had for you, not for anyone else.
- Be as clear as possible about what you would like to see repeated or done differently.
- Offer support if needed.

Good feedback is timely, clear and actionable. It is provided consistently and addresses both positive and negative behaviours and their impacts. The more you practise giving feedback in this way the more it becomes second nature.

I think this quote from Steven Levitt sums up the real value of feedback for ourselves and for others: *"The key to learning is feedback. It is nearly impossible to learn anything without it."*

You need feedback in order to become a great leader. Your team members also need feedback in order to be successful in work, to hit targets, and to know that they have been noticed for their achievements and are valued.

And your peers, manager and other stakeholders will also value constructive feedback to help them improve.

NB: I have focused in this chapter on general behavioural feedback. If you are dealing with a serious performance issue the same guidelines apply. But in those cases, you will need to be more specific about the changes you expect, timelines and consequences. Seek support from Human Resources as there are often legal requirements in these situations.

CHAPTER FIVE
ACCEPTANCE

"Acceptance is being in the moment without necessarily agreeing with it. It's about facing reality rather than trying to control it."

– Unknown

If there is one lesson I have learned that has made a dramatic difference to my energy, my ability to lead with empathy and calmness, and my enjoyment of life, it is the lesson of acceptance. Learning to accept yourself, your circumstances, and others for who they are, will enable you to live a happier, more fulfilling life. This in turn will help you to be a stronger, more engaging and supportive leader to others.

Acceptance is the antidote to frustration. It is almost impossible to feel frustrated when you accept something. As we discussed in the last chapter, when you are frustrated, you will not show up at your best, even if your intentions are good.

For me, acceptance starts with recognising what I can and can't control, and then accepting those things that are not in my control for what they are. This allows me to see things as an opportunity to learn rather than as a hindrance, frustration or barrier. When I started to accept things that were not in my control and not fight against them or expect them to be different, my level of frustration was markedly reduced.

Recognising that someone always acts in a certain way, expecting them to act differently, and then being frustrated because they don't, is a great example of folly. This is like being frustrated because the weather is bad. I have no control over the weather. It just is. When I accept the weather, I can still make choices about what I want to do in different weather conditions. I may have to change my plans or my clothing choices. But being annoyed about it only damages me and minimises the joy I could get by doing something else.

There is a Buddhist quote: *"Serenity comes when you trade expectations for acceptance."* I have certainly found this to be true. One of my most difficult lessons in acceptance was dealing with my son's mental health challenges. As a parent, it was incredibly painful to see my adult son struggling with serious depression, anxiety, and suicidal thinking. My feelings of responsibility to help him were almost overwhelming. It was only when I accepted that I could not control his choices or actions, and I could only be there to love and support him, that I regained some sense of peace.

This peace enabled me to be present for my son in a way I had not been able to before. I stopped worrying about potential outcomes and decided to just be with him in each moment. I let go of trying to control him and his choices, even though this was a very scary thing to do. This journey was not easy. I am incredibly grateful that now, after many years of struggles, my son is in a much better place.

You have probably heard some version of the Serenity Prayer: *"God, grant me the serenity to accept the things I cannot change, courage to change the things I can, and the wisdom to know the difference."* This summarises acceptance for me. There are lots of things I can control. Most importantly, I can control how I respond – to other people, and to circumstances and situations. I can take accountability for my own actions regardless of the circumstances, rather than blaming others or looking for excuses to explain my actions. And I can look for the opportunity to learn from whatever situation I am in.

This means suspending the tendency to judge. It means seeing people, events and situations as they are, without judgement, acknowledging them just as they are. Every interaction or situation you encounter is an opportunity for you to learn – about yourself, your strengths and weaknesses, and about difference, which is something to be valued rather than judged.

Choosing to try and live from a place of acceptance will open your eyes to new and different approaches. It will give you an increased sense of the value of diversity and will help you to see and draw out the best in others.

Why Is Acceptance Important?

I could write screeds on my experiences of the benefits of acceptance, but instead, let me share insights from a couple of experts. Mo Gawdat has written a book, *Solve for Happy*, in which he shares his equation for happiness: Happiness is equal to or greater than your perception of the events of your life minus your expectations of how life should be. This almost mathematical equation really resonates for me and reflects how much our expectations impact us. It is also linked to the level of frustration I mentioned in the last chapter. Understanding my expectations helped me to accept the situations I was facing and the people I was meeting, without judgement. This acceptance greatly reduced my frustration.

The Journal of Social Cognitive and Affective Neuroscience published an article in November 2019 titled *"Let it be: mindful acceptance down-regulates pain and negative emotion"*. This article summarises a study by Hedy Kober and others where participants were exposed to different stimuli. Participants were either asked to react naturally or to practise mindful acceptance. Those that practised mindful acceptance reported a reduced negative response and brain scans demonstrated notably less reactivity in the amygdala, the part of the brain that processes fear and other strong emotions.

When we face difficult situations, we can get stuck in our, often painful, emotional response. This holds us back and can be debilitating to our mental health. In simple terms, moving to acceptance, whatever our circumstances, helps us to focus on dealing with the situation in a proactive and positive way. It is not always easy to do, but the faster you can move to acceptance the faster you will move ahead.

While writing this book I have had my own struggle with acceptance. I was looking after my two-year-old grand-daughter, who was clambering on some rocks. At one point she pushed back into me, and we fell. In protecting her, I managed to break my arm. I did it well. Today, after six weeks in a cast, my arm is still swollen and not very useful. I am having regular physiotherapy but have been told it will take twelve to eighteen months to come right and I may not get my full mobility back. It has been tempting to wallow in self-pity, and in all honesty, I have had a couple of bad days. Accepting what is and focusing on whatever progress I am making, rather than obsessing over what may or may not be the eventual outcome is helping me to maintain a positive mindset and focus on the little progressions I am making each day. This is motivating me to keep improving.

Self-Acceptance

Living from a place of acceptance starts with accepting yourself. You are an imperfect human being. You have wonderful strengths and there will be things you wish you hadn't done or said, and things you would love to change about yourself. You are who you are, with all your wonder-fulness and with all your foibles. When you are able to accept yourself for who you are, you give yourself grace when you make mistakes and give yourself the space to learn and grow.

This doesn't mean taking a 'this is who I am – take me or leave me' type of mindset. I firmly believe we should constantly strive to be the best version of ourselves that we can be. But doing this from a place of acceptance means we are kind to ourselves as we grow. The key is that defining the best version of yourself is up to you, and not about the expectations of others. This kind of self-acceptance helps you to hear feedback without beating yourself up.

You have been shaped by a lifetime of experiences. The family you grew up with, the education you had, your friends, illnesses, positive and negative events have all shaped the person you are today. And like it or not, you cannot change those events. You can only accept that they happened and choose how you want to be, because of them, not in spite of them. That is the valuable learning that creates acceptance. How you respond is a choice, and it is incredibly empowering to recognise that. It gives a sense of control, even when the circumstance seems to be beyond your control. Ultimately, it means you have accountability for how you respond and the impact that response has on others.

I do not want to minimise here the impact of serious abuse or trauma by suggesting it is a simple matter to choose an empowering response. It may take years of therapy and support to truly find resolution for these types of situation. However, the consistent theme I hear from those who go on not just to survive these types of trauma, but to thrive, is a theme of taking the learning from the situation, processing it, including grieving, recognising their strengths and survival strategies, and eventually reaching acceptance and letting go.

When you become more comfortable with who you are, you are more comfortable for others to be around. This creates the conditions for others to feel more comfortable and accepted for who they are and encourages an environment where people feel able to try new things. Creativity and innovation flourish, and learning and growth take place.

When you accept yourself, you are less likely to fear failure. You will instead see endless opportunities to learn and grow. I have, unfortunately, seen many highly talented people sabotage their careers because they fear failure. When you fear failure, you tend to work yourself extremely hard and fret over every detail. This will bring great success for a while. But the more senior you become, the less control you will have and your need to avoid failing could result in you placing huge pressure on your team, poring over every detail and limiting the growth and development of your team members. Eventually, the pressure is likely to become overwhelming and you, or members of your team, may succumb to burnout. Accepting yourself, acknowledging your strengths and the areas in which you are less strong, and giving yourself grace when things don't go as you planned, enables you to focus on continual improvement instead.

Accepting Others

Every person on this planet is unique. We all have strengths and weaknesses. We all have different gifts to offer. Accepting others for who they are is a key to inclusion. We often have a fixed idea of what 'acceptable' looks like. We look for people who are like us or who fit the norms that we have experienced. In a work environment, this can mean hiring a lot of people with a similar background, who think and act in similar ways. It is certainly easier to manage a homogeneous group like this. But there are significant drawbacks. Diversity of thought, experience and background all help a team to be more innovative and open to learning. By looking for the value that individuals can bring, you create many opportunities for growth, for yourself and for the individuals around you.

When my son, who has Asperger's Syndrome, started school at age five we started to see a lot of negative behaviour changes in him. It was only after he changed schools that I realised what had been happening. The teacher in his new school saw and valued him for who he was as an individual, overlooking his quirks. She drew out his natural intelligence and created a space for him to thrive. The teacher in his previous school instead focused on trying to get him to conform to her established norms. This created huge stresses for him resulting in him acting out and becoming aggressive.

Through the course of his life, I have seen this play out over and over. When people see past his eccentricities, they see his passion for others, his heart to help and support those in need and his love for the environment and the world around him. In these environments, he thrives and makes a hugely positive contribution.

Of course, in a work environment certain requirements need to be met. But we often create unnecessary limitations by not challenging established norms. I have always been a supporter of helping women to grow in the workplace. I caught myself several years ago assuming that certain positions could not be done part-time. This was limiting the options for women who didn't want to work full-time after returning from parental leave. Once I thought about this, I started challenging my own thinking and switched my mental process from 'this can't be done part-time' to 'what would it take to enable this role to be managed part-time'? This opened my eyes to alternatives I would not have considered previously and created options that were not available before.

A colleague of mine recently shared how they had used this type of reframing to help them deal with a very challenging family situation. By stepping back and thinking about what it would take for them to make some big changes, they were able to identify the few, critical actions that unlocked possibilities for them. She was excited to share how much progress this had helped them to make. I now try to make 'what would it take...' more of a default position whenever I find myself thinking something can't work.

This idea of 'what would it take' is a simple example of reframing. Reframing is a great tool to help unlock a situation whenever you feel stuck. Stepping back to consider other perspectives, challenging the stories you have created about a specific situation and considering others' perspectives are all good ways to reframe. This process can help you to better understand what you are thinking and feeling and can help you to see things in a new way. This can be very helpful in reaching acceptance.

Acceptance is not passive and is not blind. Acceptance doesn't mean tolerating poor performance or abusive behaviour. Rather, it allows you to address the behaviour or performance without judging the person. You can accept the choices another person makes while acknowledging the consequences of those choices. If someone's work does not meet expectations, the consequences will be disciplinary action. If someone behaves abusively or consistently drains energy, the consequence could be that you choose not to spend time with them.

In both instances, you can be explicit about the behaviour, its impact and the consequences if it does not change, without judging the individual. You can even offer support or coaching if appropriate. Then it is up to the other person to decide how to respond.

Acceptance in the Business

The same logic applies to decisions that may be made in your organisation that you don't agree with. Even in very senior roles, there will always be someone you have to answer to who may make a choice that is different from yours. If, after constructive discussion, the decision is made and is outside of your control, you really have only two choices:

1. Accept the decision and move on – even if you disagree with the decision you will need to support its implementation.
2. If you cannot accept the decision, particularly if it crosses a value for you or puts you in a legal or ethical bind, then choose to leave the situation.

Any alternatives amount to resistance of some form and will only end up draining your energy, and likely impacting your performance, and potentially the performance of your team and others around you. I am not suggesting you just blindly accept any decision that is made without debate. To return to the principles in the chapter on listening, I encourage open discussion to fully understand the rationale, balanced discussion of your counterproposals, and even good, healthy debate.

Good teams and businesses encourage disagreement and debate. It is key to delivering strong business outcomes, and to creating an innovative and creative environment. The trick is to know when to stop and accept that the decision is made. I am sure you have seen people continue to argue long after it is clear the decision is made. This is seldom to their benefit. Consider the old question, "Is this worth dying on your sword for?" when deciding how long and how hard to fight.

Acceptance and Control

As discussed at the beginning of this chapter, acceptance starts with understanding what we can control. In *The Seven Habits of Highly Effective People*, Stephen Covey talks about three levels of circles:

1. The Circle of Concern: Things that impact us where we have no influence on the outcome.
2. The Circle of Influence: Things we can influence but don't directly control.
3. The Circle of Control: What we directly control through our thoughts, words and actions.

Understanding these three circles is key to moving to acceptance. When you expend a lot of energy on things you have no control over, or you try to influence things you may be concerned about but really need to accept, this is very draining and wastes a lot of time that you could spend better on much more productive things.

Trying to do others' jobs, and stressing over other people's lives or their decisions is another waste of energy. Here your role is simply to provide an informed point of view and support. Save your energy and focus your time and actions to make the biggest impact where you actually can.

It is not always easy to let go and accept. I often find myself thinking about things that are outside of my control. These days, I am quicker to recognise that and quicker to let go and move on. It is harder for me to let go of things that seem closer to me, issues that affect my family members or close friends. Remembering these circles of control helps me to know that I am not responsible for others' choices or actions. It makes it easier for me to love unconditionally, to support their choices, and to focus on living my own life to the best of my ability.

Putting Acceptance Into Practice

Build awareness of your thoughts and emotions. Being mindful helps a lot in this process. Some people find journalling or meditation helps.

Accept yourself. Embrace all the things that make you unique. Acknowledge and let go of the things you don't control – stay in the present. Be kind to yourself and quiet your inner critic. Think about how you would support or encourage a friend or colleague and try and 'talk' to yourself the same way.

Think about where you spend your time and energy. Catch yourself when you begin to focus on things you can't control and shift your focus to the things you can.

Challenge any perceptions or ideas that may limit you or others. Think 'what would it take...'

Check your expectations. Where have they come from? Are they realistic and reasonable? Have you communicated them effectively to others? Unrealistic expectations set you up for frustration, which works against acceptance.

This quote from Tony Robbins is a good way to sum up this chapter: *"Acceptance is not weakness; it is a strength that allows us to grow and evolve."* The more you learn to accept yourself and your circumstances, the more you will grow. As you grow and evolve as a leader you will support your team members to grow and evolve also, ultimately leading to stronger results.

CHAPTER SIX
RESPONSIBILITY

"Man must cease attributing his problems to his environment, and again learn to exercise his will – his personal responsibility."

– Albert Einstein

Learning and growth happen when you take responsibility for your actions and responses. It is easy to make excuses and to see faults in others. It is often harder to examine yourself and see how you are contributing to the situation. Responsibility is about owning your actions and responses and recognising how they impact those around you and the results you deliver.

I learned a very important leadership lesson about responsibility when I was the General Manager of an Australian business. Quality was incredibly important to the business, and I was also passionate about it. I talked about quality regularly and encouraged people to make it a priority. I was devastated when the business failed a quality audit. It didn't go down too well at head office either. We quickly identified some changes that needed to be made. Our quality processes were being managed by one person and weren't well documented. We were ready to fix the issue and move on.

Our global quality expert came to visit to review our progress. As we sat in the boardroom sharing our learnings, he gently stopped me and said, "If, in your analysis of the issues, you have not found something that you, around this table, are responsible for, you have not gone deep enough."

Wow! I was taken aback. It was a confronting thought. We thought we had been clear about who bore the responsibility and we had identified actions to rectify the issue. But, after a little reflection, I realised that it wasn't enough for me to be passionate about quality. I was not actively focusing on the quality processes and reinforcing the need for consistent adherence. Yes, the issues we had identified were real and needed to be addressed. But, unless I, as the leader of the organisation, changed the way I communicated quality and the questions I asked, we would likely fall into the same trap in the future.

This lesson has stayed with me. Whatever proportion of responsibility others bear in an outcome, I try to reflect on the part I have played. How have my words or actions positively or negatively impacted the results we are seeing? What might I be doing that inadvertently rewards or reinforces behaviours that are not the ones we want. How else might I be contributing to the situation?

This does not diminish the responsibility of others. Sometimes people make mistakes or let you down. But if your first instinct is always to see the fault in others, you may miss your contribution to the situation. This is particularly important as a leader. Before you address someone's poor performance, ask yourself:

- Have you made your expectations of performance clear?
- Have you provided the training, resources and tools needed to deliver the desired outcome?
- Have you created an environment where people can ask for help when they need it?
- What behaviours and outcomes are you reinforcing, intentionally or not?

You will face circumstances beyond your control, and these may negatively impact your results. Allowing yourself to become a victim of your circumstances may be tempting, but it does not empower you. And it will not help you to improve your results. In situations like this, acknowledge the reality. It is what it is. Then ask yourself:

- What can I do now, within this context, to improve our performance?
- How could I positively impact the circumstances?
- Who might be able to help?

This last question is important. A valuable lesson in leadership is that taking responsibility doesn't mean you have to do it alone. In fact, enrolling others to support becomes increasingly important. The more senior you become, the less you do on your own, the more you need to empower your team, and the more you need to engage your peers and stakeholders in support.

Taking Responsibility for Your Actions

Your actions matter. In any position, you have responsibilities and need to deliver results. If you say you are going to do something, do it. If you find you are no longer able to do what you said, then it is crucial to communicate that. You will not maintain your success if you do not meet your commitments. Part of being responsible is knowing what you can actually deliver. It might be tempting to say yes to an important request or project, but if you do not have the time, resources or capability to deliver, you will let yourself and the business down. It is far better to be honest about your workload and manage expectations upfront. You may be able to negotiate a different time frame, or a different priority for some of your other work.

Over-committing to work projects and then needing to take responsibility for following through on delivery can have a negative impact on your work-life balance, and often on the work-life balance of your team. This is a slippery slope, and you can easily end up compromising some of your personal boundaries if you do not get this under control. Think carefully before agreeing to take on work.

One way to avoid inadvertently over-committing is to take a few minutes to get clear on the expectations before you agree to do something. Asking a few questions before you get started can save a lot of time, energy and effort on rework later:

- What will success look like?
- When is it required?
- What format is it needed in?
- Who else needs to be involved – and are they available?

- Are there other interdependencies to be aware of?
- Is there any context available that would help you to better understand this request?

Consider carefully how much time the commitment will require and manage expectations around timing to ensure it is feasible. As a leader, your actions speak far louder than your words. The more senior you are, the more carefully people watch what you do. What you say carries much less meaning. If you talk about the importance of punctuality but then show up late for every meeting, your team will soon learn to do the same. By contrast, if you start meetings on time, whether everyone is there or not, you will soon find that everyone is there, ready to go when the session is due to start.

Be intentional about the things that are important to you and think about the example you set. If you consistently over-commit and don't meet deadlines your team will likely act the same way. If you talk about work-life balance but work all hours of the day and night to deliver, they will do the same – or they will look for work elsewhere, in a place their personal boundaries are not crossed.

Taking Responsibility for Your Reactions

Taking responsibility for yourself is about how you respond, regardless of the situation. I think Viktor E. Frankl expresses this well when he states: *"Between stimulus and response there is space. In that space is our power to choose our response. In our response lies growth and freedom."*

Whilst it can be uncomfortable, recognising that you always have a choice about how to respond is freeing. You are not controlled by other people's words or behaviours, or by situations. You have the freedom to decide how to respond. The choices you make will determine the impact you have.

If you have little children, you have probably heard them say something like, "So and so made me do it," as a way to avoid punishment for something they did. This is pretty easy to see through. And yet, as we get older, we often hold other people responsible for the way we feel and react. Taking responsibility for ourselves means owning our own emotions. Changing the way we frame things makes a big difference. Think about the difference between the following two sentences:

1. *You make me so mad when...*
2. *I feel mad when you...*

The first statement puts all the responsibility for you being mad on the other person. It suggests you have absolutely no alternative but to be mad. Because it is accusatory, it is also more likely to result in a defensive response from the other party. Things could escalate rapidly. The second statement takes ownership of the feeling. It still gives space for the other's behaviour or action to be addressed.

The difference between these two statements may seem like semantics, but words do matter. When you take responsibility for how you respond to a stimulus, you take back power for yourself. Importantly, by being present in the moment and acknowledging your emotional response, you give yourself the space to choose to respond differently. As a leader, role modelling this type of personal responsibility creates a space for others to also own their responses, and to learn and grow.

It is worth understanding that your feelings come from your beliefs or your expectations, which come from your life experience or what you've been taught. When you remind yourself that you are, at some level, choosing your feelings, then you can look at the hierarchy and see where that choice has come from, and what you can do to change your beliefs or expectations. In other words, you can take responsibility for yourself. You can't change your life experience, but you can challenge what you've been taught.

Bringing this to life, the second example above could read: I (choose to) feel mad when you... The 'I choose' is a reminder to take responsibility for the feeling. It is important not to judge the choice. There is nothing wrong with choosing to feel mad, or frustrated, or any other feeling, but understanding what triggers that helps you to take responsibility for being clearer about your expectations, or changing your beliefs about the expected outcome.

One of the biggest mistakes we make in our thinking is expecting others to react and respond the same way we do. Understanding that others' reactions will come from their feelings, based on their beliefs or expectations, can remind you not to judge their impact but to dig deeper to understand their intent. Seeking to understand intent, rather than judging impact, or reacting in an emotional way, will help you to create a sense of psychological safety. This will help you to draw out the best from your team members, peers and others that you deal with.

Supporting the Responsibility of Others

One of the best things you can do to encourage the growth of your team is to be clear about your expectations and give them the space to deliver. This does not mean abdicating your responsibility to provide support. But, if you micro-manage by diving into the details and monitoring every step, this does not give your team members the opportunity to learn and grow. Micro-managing can have a very negative impact on your team, shutting down creativity and learning. It also means you essentially hold the direct responsibility for getting every detail right, which can be very tiring.

Always aiming for perfection can be very limiting. In many situations, it is much more freeing to aim for progress over perfection - for you and for your team. Learning to trust your team and giving them the space to explore their own creative ideas is very empowering, even if it can be challenging to let go, especially if the team's ideas are different from yours.

In fact, letting go and allowing your team members to make choices, even if you think they are wrong, will create great learning opportunities. You will need to judge the level of risk you are prepared to take and manage the cost of potential mistakes. Consider the seniority and experience of your team members and their capabilities. Gradually increase the amount of freedom you give them. Sometimes you may be surprised when something you thought wouldn't work actually turns out to be better than your own idea. This is definitely something I have experienced.

Context Before Content

One thing I have found very powerful as a leader, and that has helped me to let go more, is providing context. I used to focus on providing content, giving people all the specifics, without providing the bigger picture. This sometimes led to confusion. People didn't understand the reason for the work they were being asked to do, or how it affected the broader organisation. This could result in rework because critical interfaces were missed.

I developed a mantra: 'Context before Content' to help me remember to frame requests by first providing the background. My team found this much more empowering. By understanding the background and the reason for requests, they were much more likely to be motivated to deliver high quality work.

I remember a wise team member of mine commenting once that people who are more senior always have more perspective. I didn't fully acknowledge this at the time, but I now know it to be true. As you become more senior, you have a much greater overview of how the business operates and how all the different pieces work together. Providing relevant background context will help your team to learn, and to make better business choices. I have found this to be particularly helpful when driving big change initiatives. The more I have been able to provide the rationale for the change at a broader organisation level, the better my team has been able to accept and embrace the change, even if they didn't like the impact it had on them personally.

Peter Block, an Organisational Psychologist, says that if you have no opportunity to say no, your yes is meaningless. Providing context helps the team to understand why a decision has been made, and giving your team members the permission and the space to express their concerns and fears helps them to accept the decision. Giving them time to reflect, and hearing and acknowledging their concerns in an empathetic way, especially when a change has been mandated and is out of their control, allows the team to move to acceptance more readily.

Responsibility and Development

Your role as a leader in helping others develop is a bit like being a mirror. Your responsibility is not to control how another person behaves or performs. Neither is it to judge what is causing their behaviour. Strategically drawing their attention to the impact of their behaviour or performance, and spelling out any implications, creates the opportunity for their self-reflection and growth. You can provide support and coaching as requested but avoid the temptation to give lots of advice. Remember to own your observations – as referenced in Chapter Four on Feedback.

Early in your career you were an individual contributor and needed to become an expert at what you did. You may have been expected to have all the answers about your area of expertise. As a leader, your role is much more about having powerful questions than it is about having answers. This won't necessarily stop people coming to ask you for answers, so you will need to be intentional.

Peter Block expresses this well: "*Questions open the door to the future and are more powerful than answers in that they demand engagement.*" The simple question, *what do you think?* is a great starting point. When you practise asking this question whenever someone comes to you for advice, it creates an immediate pause. This encourages the other person to think and reflect, and it helps to stop you from immediately leaping to give advice. Asking questions rather than providing answers encourages others to take responsibility for finding their own solutions. It creates the space for their reflection and personal growth. Supporting the responsibility of others extends beyond your team to your peers, your boss and other stakeholders. Open questions, when asked in a supportive environment, encourage reflection and growth, and they can work with everyone.

Here are a few of my favourite questions for opening up discussion and encouraging reflection:

- What is possible?
- What is your contribution to the situation?
- What risks are you prepared to take?
- What doubts and reservations do you have?
- What, in this situation, has meaning for you?
- What struck you (about a conversation or activity)?
- What is the payoff for you? or What is it costing you?

In short, responsibility is a way of life, whether you are taking responsibility for your own actions and reactions, or encouraging and supporting others to be responsible for their learning and growth. Christopher Avery, from The Responsibility Company, sums up responsibility nicely: *"Taking responsibility is a commitment to own your life, self-leadership, growth and freedom."*

Responsibility means taking ownership for your choices and for the results you deliver. It means not giving up when things get difficult but continually seeking new ways to meet your commitments. Responsible leaders are valued by the business and respected by their teams.

CHAPTER SEVEN
VALUING DIFFERENCE

"Good leadership requires you to surround yourself with people of diverse perspectives who can disagree with you without fear of retaliation."

– Doris Kearns Goodwin

Every individual is unique and brings different experiences and perspectives to whatever they do. Actively seeking out different opinions, perspectives and ideas will strengthen your thinking, help you make better decisions and help you deliver more consistent results. If you surround yourself with people of similar backgrounds, who all think and act the same way you do, you are likely to miss opportunities.

I have been privileged to work with people from multiple cultures, countries and ethnicities. I have learned to value the strength that diversity brings to a team and to an organisation. In my last role, I was responsible for about one hundred countries and led a team that spanned sixteen time zones, with my direct reports representing fourteen different nationalities.

And this was just the start of the differences between us. It is not always easy to reach alignment with such a diverse team, but I loved the experience. One of the things I loved most was learning about the different backgrounds of each person and understanding more about their cultures and beliefs. It is very easy to fall into the trap of expecting other people to think, act and respond the same way that we do. This is unrealistic and invariably leads to frustration or conflict. *The Culture Map*, by Erin Meyer, is a fantastic book to help understand diverse cultures. It looks at different dimensions and identifies where we are more and less alike. I found it very helpful to keep this book in mind when I was struggling to understand the way someone approached or responded to a situation.

Beyond working multi-culturally, valuing difference is a key contributor to creativity and innovation, and it leads to improved decision making and risk management. You can only know what you know, and you can only see the world through the lens of your own experience. It is very easy to start thinking that your views are the only right ones. Actively seeking diverse perspectives can open your eyes to new ideas. This is becoming increasingly important in today's environment where social media algorithms tend to feed us information that reinforces our own perspectives. Actively seeking divergent views can help to ensure that you look at issues from all sides.

Senior leaders are often confronted with complex and difficult decisions. I use the analogy of a brilliant-cut diamond when I think about the multiple perspectives that might be at play. Different people in a team may consider an issue from their own perspective which is like looking through only one facet of the diamond. When you try to consider all the perspectives of an issue, this helps you to come up with the best, or in some cases, the least-worst, solution to the issue. The more strongly you hold a view, the more important it is to check that you have not missed something important. Remember that more than one thing can be true. You may well be right, but it never hurts to check.

Proactively seeking diverse input can also help guard against blind spots. In 2020, during the Black Lives Matter movement, our business was proactively exploring diversity. One of my team members, who is of non-white ethnicity, sent me an email saying how excited he was about this, and hoping that someone would look at the M&M characters. My initial reaction was that he must be joking. After all, the M&M characters are all different colours. I decided to check in on what he meant. He explained that the arms and legs of all the characters are 'white' flesh coloured. I was completely taken aback. I had never noticed this before. It was an excellent reminder that we take so many things for granted, especially if they reinforce our own stereotypes or beliefs.

Acceptance, listening and vulnerability, discussed in previous chapters, are foundational to the ability to effectively recognise, value and incorporate diverse views and perspectives. This is not just about being nice. There is plenty of research that suggests that well-managed, diverse teams deliver stronger results.

Difference and Development

Just as we all have different experiences and perspectives, there are also many different styles and preferences for learning. Some people are very hands on and learn through doing, others like to read information, some prefer to understand all the background, some only want to understand the task, and others prefer to watch videos, or be shown step-by-step what to do.

Understanding the ways in which people learn and absorb information is important when developing training materials, induction programs, or communicating important information. When you only consider your own learning style and preferences you may be surprised when some people miss important content. Well-designed programs will cater to multiple preferences to maximise learning. This becomes increasingly important when communicating critical information like safety requirements.

Equally, each individual deserves a development plan that reflects their unique strengths, ambitions and needs. It can be tempting to simplify your approach to development or career planning and apply the same approach for everyone. This is unlikely to deliver the best results. Understanding your team members' desires, motivations, personal situations and strengths enables you to support them to craft a personalised development plan that is targeted specifically to them. Start with understanding their aspirations. Consider the following questions:

- What do they want to achieve?
- What experiences, capabilities and drivers do they have that support their ambitions?
- What gaps might they have?

- What experiences could help them to close those gaps? (Projects, Roles, etc.)
- Who can they learn from? (Role models, peers, mentors, coaches)
- What education or training might be required?

Considering different learning styles and targeting development to the needs of each individual will help ensure you maximise the potential of your team. Ultimately, this will help you to deliver stronger results.

Personality Preferences

You have probably come across some sort of personality assessment, like Myers-Briggs or Hogan. These assessments are helpful in identifying your preferences for how you think, where you get your energy, and how you process information. In a team environment, it can be useful to understand each others' preferences on the different dimensions. It is important, though, to remember that these instruments only measure preference. Your choices are not set in stone.

For example, I have a strong preference for introvert versus extrovert behaviour. I need some quiet time to maintain my energy. In fact, I find social situations extremely uncomfortable and tiring. In a leadership position, I could not always avoid these situations. I adapted my behaviour to suit. I found this fairly easy in a business setting, but I still found attending a lot of social events to be very tiring. I managed this by being open and setting boundaries.

In my last role, I travelled extensively. I set a guideline for my team that I would be fully present and available all day. I was happy to do breakfast meetings, lunch meetings and town hall presentations or customer meetings. But I limited my evening engagements to two a week. This balance gave me the space I needed to re-energise so I could show up at my best the rest of the time. Some of the extroverts in my team wanted to get out and socialise every evening because this is where they re-energised. By being clear upfront about our preferences, we were able to accommodate everyone's needs without judgement.

It can be a useful team exercise to take one of the personality style assessments. Understanding your own and others' preferences can help each of you to set and communicate boundaries. This type of mutual understanding can help the team to function better and build tolerance for differences.

Thinking Preferences

Having people in the team with different preferences for thinking styles can be extremely helpful. Some people prefer to think conceptually. They are interested in the big picture, in patterns and ideas. Others prefer the concrete – things they can see and feel, and tend to think more linearly. Both are valid and equally valuable. Understanding your own preferences and those of others helps you to draw out different perspectives.

NB: Thinking preferences are also included in general style preference assessments.

When you view a problem only through your own lens, you may miss valuable information. If you work with a team of people who all have similar backgrounds and thinking styles, it becomes even more important to proactively seek out alternate views. This will help you avoid 'groupthink'. Groupthink happens when a group of people prioritise consensus over critical thinking in decision making. It can be dangerous as it can result in vital information or critical process gaps being missed.

Encouraging dissenting voices is a very useful way to overcome this. In fact, because of the risk, the more your team aligns behind a single view the more important it is to seek an alternative view. This may or may not change your decision in the long run, but it will help you ensure that you have not missed anything important.

It is not always easy to speak up if your view differs from everyone else's. As a leader, you set the tone of the discussion. Actively requesting alternative views and praising people who raise concerns will help you create an environment where people feel more comfortable. The more you do this, the more dynamic your team discussions will become. This may seem counterintuitive or inefficient. But the time invested in this process will save you dollars and time in the long run.

Every year we used to conduct a peer review of the Operating Plans for the following year. Each General Manager would present their team's plan to the rest of the regional team. The team would listen and provide feedback on what they saw as strengths and what they thought might be missing. Because of the time zone differences, we conducted these sessions over a week. At the end of each day, we checked in to see how it was working so we could adjust, to ensure the process was valuable for everyone.

I have a vivid memory of a session a few years ago. At the end of the first day, everyone was providing positive feedback about how it was working. It is always tempting to stop with the positive feedback. Things must be working. But I wanted to be sure. I checked in one more time and asked if there was anything we could do to improve. One of the General Managers made an excellent suggestion for how we could better engage the local team members involved in preparing the Operating Plans. If I had not kept encouraging a dissenting voice, we would have missed a great opportunity to improve our process. This is just one very simple example to illustrate the potential.

I could list many, many situations where having alternative viewpoints in the discussion has helped us get a better outcome. Many years ago, we were planning a new product launch in the New Zealand business. The team was excited about the launch and working together on the plans.

During a team discussion, we checked in again to see if we had missed anything. One person mentioned that they were concerned about how we were planning to phase in the changes. They had been worried about it for a while but had not wanted to say anything because everyone else seemed happy with what was planned. I was very glad they spoke up. It resulted in us revisiting what we had planned and helped us to avoid some significant stock shortages, ultimately ensuring the success of the product launch.

Unconscious Bias

There is a lot of information available about bias and the impact it has. Harvard University defines unconscious bias as: *"unintended, subtle, and subconscious associations learned through past experiences. Thoughts that happen to all of us, that we are unaware of on a conscious level."* Harvard has also developed an online test you can take to identify your biases. I found taking some of these tests quite enlightening.

As a leader, it is important to consider bias when recruiting, building teams and managing performance. The more you expose yourself to different cultures, perspectives and experiences, the more you will be likely to expand your thinking and minimise bias. Seeking diverse viewpoints will also help.

I am not an expert in this and I encourage you to learn more. The Harvard Implicit Bias test is available at: https://implicit.harvard.edu/implicit/takeatouchtest.html. There are numerous good books on this subject as well. In the meantime, here are a few keys for minimising bias when recruiting:

- First review job descriptions. Check for language that may be exclusive. Are the criteria and job requirements valid?
- Conduct 'blind' resume checks where possible. Recruiters can help with this and there are also software programs available. These checks focus on the education and experience of the candidate and take out unconscious bias on the basis of names and other gender or cultural cues.
- Conduct structured interviews. Standardised questions help you to focus on the competencies you have pre-determined to be most important to the role you are hiring for.
- Be especially wary about focusing too much on how well the person will 'fit' in your organisation. While motivational alignment is important, placing too much emphasis on this dimension is likely to result in you hiring a lot of people who are very similar.

Inclusion

Building a diverse team is a great start. But if you then expect everyone on the team to conform to a narrow range of behaviour, you will miss out on the value of that diversity. And you will likely find that you have a high rate of turnover. Verna Myers puts this well when she says, *"Diversity is being asked to the party; inclusion is being asked to dance."*

Inclusion means giving space for the differences that we all have. It starts with understanding. Assumptions are what get us into trouble. The best way to build understanding is through having a conversation. If you are unsure of someone's preferences, ask in a genuinely curious way, without judgement. This will create the space for mutual understanding.

Some simple things that encourage inclusion:

- Be yourself – your authenticity and vulnerability will encourage the same from those around you.
- Invite everyone to speak up. In team meetings be aware of those that have not provided an opinion and ask if they have anything to add.
- Actively listen to hear different viewpoints.
- Challenge stereotypes and clamp down on any non-inclusive behaviour in your team.
- Proactively seek feedback.
- Consider educational opportunities.

I am also a big fan of one-to-one conversations. In all my leadership roles I have made it a priority to make time to connect individually with my team members on a regular basis. This has allowed me to get to know them better and to understand what is important to them and how they like to work. Creating an inclusive workplace means allowing people to be themselves. This means they are free to spend their energy on driving business performance instead of pretending to be something they aren't. It also creates the opportunity for everyone on the team to stretch their own perspectives and learn new approaches.

Given the challenges today in recruiting and retaining talent, it is important to have as broad a pool as possible. When you create a diverse and inclusive environment that allows people to be themselves, and when you accommodate different needs with flexibility and without judgement, you give yourself the best opportunity to attract the best talent. Max DePree, in *Leadership is an Art* expresses this very well: *"We need to give each other the space to grow, to be ourselves, to exercise our diversity. We need to give each other space so that we may both give and receive such beautiful things as ideas, openness, dignity, joy, healing, and inclusion."*

In summary, building an inclusive, diverse team will help you to attract and retain great talent. It will also encourage better innovation and creativity, help you to avoid group-think and lead to better business outcomes. Diverse teams may not be as straightforward to manage as homogeneous ones, but the advantages are numerous. In today's world, being an effective leader absolutely requires this skill.

CHAPTER EIGHT

CULTIVATING CURIOSITY AND CONTINUOUS LEARNING

"Remember that things are not always as they appear to be. Curiosity creates possibilities and opportunities."

– Roy T. Bennett

The world around us is constantly changing and the pace of change is accelerating exponentially. New things are being developed every day. Our political, economic and social environments are in a constant state of flux. The Covid pandemic shifted the way many of us see the world, and the development of AI is leading us into an unprecedented technological era. Unless you stay curious and keep learning you will fall behind.

Doing what you have always done, even if it was successful, will not guarantee you success in the future. Cultivating your own curiosity, and the curiosity of your team will help you to keep growing. Stretch yourself to look at things differently and challenge your own perspective. This becomes even more important when you think you know a lot about something.

I have always considered myself to be a curious person – one who thrives on learning. But I received a valuable lesson in 2016. I had been managing the Australian Petcare business for Mars, Incorporated for about six years. This business had multiple brands and operated in supermarkets and pet specialty stores with a specialty-only brand, Advance. Mars also owns a large specialty-only petcare brand, Royal Canin. I looked at the Royal Canin brand the same way as I looked at the Advance brand and didn't understand why it was managed differently.

It was only when I stepped into a global role, responsible for the Specialty Petcare strategy that my perspective changed. I began to explore more about the brand, set aside my preconceived ideas, and started to really understand the differences. I was embarrassed to realise that I had missed many opportunities to learn this much earlier by focusing on what I thought I knew instead of practising open curiosity.

I have always enjoyed attending training programs and learning new things. When I was younger, I used to only value learning things that I considered to be material or significant. I used to complain about being bored if I didn't think I was learning something new and meaningful all the time. Eventually I realised that there is a huge amount of learning in the nuance of things, and this piqued my curiosity in a new way. My mindset about learning changed. I started learning about things from a lot of different angles and perspectives instead of just gaining an overview and thinking I understood them well.

In hindsight, my attitude to learning used to be quite arrogant and I missed many opportunities because of it. Kevin Plank, the CEO of Under Armour expressed this perfectly when he said, *"I want people to believe in themselves. I want intellectual curiosity. I want someone who realises that they don't know it all and that they're dying to learn."* When you think you already know something, your curiosity shuts down.

Constantly challenge yourself on what you already know. What else could be true? Seek out people and situations that bring different perspectives. Consider all the ways you learn new things. Travel, meeting new people, trying new foods, exploring new routes, reading about different topics, listening to podcasts and watching documentaries are a few of the things that may come to mind. Every conversation is an opportunity to learn – about the person you are talking to, the subject you are talking about, and about yourself. Every activity you do and every interaction you have is an opportunity to practise curiosity and grow. Encouraging curiosity in your team members will help them grow, and will help the team to identify potential new sources of growth, or solutions to challenges.

As the world changes, staying aware of new technologies and understanding their impacts becomes increasingly important. Keep up to date with business news and seek out experts who can help you to learn.

Critical Thinking

While you are developing your curiosity it is equally important to practise critical thinking. In today's world of readily available 'information', misinformation is flourishing. Learn to check your facts and avoid making assumptions. I had a line manager very early in my career who was fond of reminding us that '*assume* just makes an ass out of you and me'. It is important to check data sources and challenge assumptions. Be curious and look for alternatives.

Continually expand your thinking and question why things are the way they are. It can be very tempting to take things at face value or to accept simple explanations. This can lead to errors of judgement and costly mistakes. It is sometimes frustrating to have to analyse all the data to get to the bottom of an issue. I remember working with the global team to try to understand some specific product attributes. It was very hard to get consistent data and very tempting to shortcut the process and make a pragmatic decision. I am very glad that sane heads prevailed. Allowing a little extra time helped us avoid making a very costly error that could have had significant business and customer impact.

Building your perspective and strengthening your business acumen will make you a stronger leader. While you do not need to have all the answers, critical thinking, combined with perspective and experience, will help you improve your judgement, come up with the right questions to ask, and will guide your decision making. I encourage you to read broadly, particularly anything related to general business, technology, your industry and leadership. You will no doubt find multiple differing points of view but combining those will help you to develop a fuller world view, which will help you tackle the complex challenges you face.

Learning and the Comfort Zone

There is a gap between knowing something and doing something. I learned this gap the hard way when I received the painful feedback about the gap between the impact I was having and my intent. I covered this in more detail in the introduction. The coach I was working with at the time was nearly as surprised as I was at the feedback I received. He stated that he had found me to be as literate in the realm of leadership and transformation as any business leader he had worked with. Knowing the theory and putting it into practice are clearly two very different things.

Making learning useful requires turning head knowledge into practical application. It requires commitment, focus and the willingness to receive and act on feedback, and to try new things. This is often uncomfortable. A previous co-worker of mine, and an expert in Learning and Development, was fond of saying, "There is no growth in the comfort zone and there is no comfort in the growth zone." I have definitely found this to be true. It is easy to say now, but learning to be comfortable with being uncomfortable has been another key step in my journey to being an effective leader.

As you become more senior, you are likely to be faced with situations you have never been in before. You have probably heard the term VUCA: volatile, uncertain, complex and ambiguous. This certainly applies to the world we live in today, and any leader will need to learn how to manage in a VUCA environment. You will have to make decisions when you do not have all the information. You will need to manage risks. You will need to support your teams when they face their own uncertainties. All of this is likely to result in a degree of discomfort. But you cannot let that stop you from moving forward. Learning to be comfortable with feeling uncomfortable enables you to keep moving forward and practising critical thinking, even when you don't have all the answers.

One of the things that helps me in these situations is an unshakeable belief that we can find a way. I have a deep belief in the human ability to figure things out and overcome obstacles. This helped me when I faced situations for which I did not have an answer. When I was a fairly new General Manager, running the business in New Zealand, I was confronted with such a situation.

I had been in the role for about nine months, and we had made great progress. We were on track to deliver a record full-year performance. As we planned for the following year, we realised that changes in the foreign exchange rate would erode nearly all the profit we had made that year. That was certainly not going to be reflected in our targets. I had no idea what to do. But I knew we could find a way.

I pulled our key leaders together and outlined the situation. I provided the context for what was happening and detailed the challenge we faced. Our targets had been set and would need to be delivered. I knew that if I unleashed the curiosity and creative power of the team, they would identify some good options. It took a lot of time and some hard work, but they did.

The team developed some really innovative plans that involved adjusting our product mix, making some targeted cost savings and some sourcing changes. All of this took many of us, including me, well outside our comfort zones. Ultimately, despite facing what initially looked like an impossible plan, we delivered another record year and set the business on a stronger trajectory for the future. Importantly, we all learned a lot through the process, about the business, about our ways of working, and about ourselves. This stood us in good stead whenever we faced problems that seemed impossible.

You do not need to wait for situations that seem impossible in order to get out of your comfort zone and to learn and grow. There are many ways you can stretch yourself to look at things differently when they initially feel uncomfortable. This can be as simple as changing the way you travel to work or as challenging as learning a brand-new skill. Exploring different beliefs and perspectives, without judgement, can also be uncomfortable, especially if they challenge something you are passionate about. They can open your eyes to new and different approaches and help you to be more accepting of others.

Encourage your team to explore from your customer's perspective. This can work for internal and external customers. It will open many insights that will help you improve your product or service offering. Think creatively about how you can set up experiences and interactions to facilitate this. Consider relevant industry groups or associations you can interact with. Who is best in class in your line of work? Challenge yourself to think outside the box here, beyond the things you have done before or are already aware of. What else might you consider?

Reflection

Peter Drucker says, *"Follow effective action with quiet reflection. From the quiet reflection will come even more effective action."* In a similar vein, John Dewey comments: *"We do not learn from experience, we learn from reflecting on experience.*" Unless you commit the time to reflect on what is and isn't working, and how you could do better, you will likely continue to do the same thing and minimise your learning. Reflection doesn't need to be a long, complicated process. You will keep progressing when you make the time regularly to think about how things are working and what you could do differently.

For yourself, take a few moments at the beginning or end of each day to reflect on your progress. What are you happy about? What do you want to do differently? Who do you need to check in with? How will you hold yourself accountable for the changes you want to make? It is important not to beat yourself up when things don't go exactly how you want them to, or when you make a mistake. Even though it is easy to fall into this trap, this type of self-flagellation is not helpful and can lead to inertia. Remind yourself that you are human and therefore not perfect. In my experience, some of my biggest breakthroughs have come from some of my biggest failures. They have led to my biggest learnings, and I would not be the leader or person I am today if I had not had those experiences.

With your team, make a habit of checking in at the end of meetings and projects. A simple reflective exercise asking people to think about what worked, and what they wish, will take only a few minutes but will set you on a path of continuous improvement. As mentioned earlier in this book, if you are getting only a whole lot of positives, recognise that and appreciate the feedback. Then ask again what could have been better. It can take people a while to feel comfortable about raising things that didn't go well. Sit with the discomfort of silence for a few moments, giving people space to respond. Avoid the temptation to rush through, or you may miss some valuable learning.

Learning and Leadership

In very simple terms, if you are not learning you will stagnate and you will not continue to be successful in the rapidly changing environment in which we live. You will limit your personal and professional growth. Without reflection, you will not learn, or at the very least, you will not recognise what you are learning and will therefore not be able to apply it consistently.

It is the application of learning that will deliver results, for you and for the business. As a leader, the best thing you can do to encourage your team members to learn is to role model curiosity and a willingness to learn yourself. In particular, acknowledging and sharing when things didn't go well for you will help your team to do the same. This will help you to create a psychologically safe workspace, which has been proven to enhance learning.

Beyond role modelling, you also have a responsibility to create an environment that encourages learning. Every leader is responsible for developing and growing talent for the future. This starts with hiring great people. Always aim to hire people who are better than you. This will make your job easier and will ensure the future proofing of the organisation. Giving those people opportunities to learn, to make mistakes, to reflect and grow, will help them develop their full potential, and will help you and your team to collectively deliver fantastic results. Ronald Regan summed this concept up well when he said, *"The greatest leader is not necessarily the one who does the greatest things. He is the one that gets the people to do the greatest things."*

Continuous learning is important. Putting that learning into practice is harder, but even more valuable. Creating the space for your team to learn takes patience and under-standing. Consistent application will help you and your team to keep growing and to deliver great results.

CHAPTER NINE
ENGAGING STAKEHOLDERS

"The new form of networking is not about climbing a ladder to success; it's about collaboration, co-creation, partnerships, and long-term values-based relationships."

– Porter Gayle

I did not initially visualise this chapter when I was thinking about writing this book. But as I reflected, I realised that at least half the people I have mentored and coached have asked questions about the interlinked topics of stakeholder engagement and networking. It was not something I thought about earlier in my career. And as an introvert, I certainly didn't network naturally. I learned the hard lesson that the more senior you become, the more you need to engage diverse stakeholders.

Early in your career, the people most responsible for your performance reviews and potential promotions are likely to be fairly close to you and have a good view of what you are doing and the impact you are having. Your work will largely speak for you and if you do a good job and show potential you will be rewarded accordingly. You may need to collaborate with some co-workers and a small group of interested parties but generally, the value of what you do will be easy to see.

As you get more senior, the people responsible for assessing your performance and managing your promotion are likely to be further removed. As you become more autonomous, they are less likely to have a detailed understanding of what you are doing. Also, there will probably be more of them, and they are likely to have more diverse backgrounds, especially if you are in a large, multinational organisation.

This was certainly the case for me. Early in my career, while I no doubt missed some opportunities to proactively network, it didn't hold me back. When I took my first General Management role, I was leading the New Zealand business. While the business was sizeable in New Zealand terms, it was a small contributor to the regional business. Therefore, my goal, and my contract with my boss, the Regional President, was that we would be the business he didn't need to worry about. We would get on and deliver what was expected, and I would give him a heads-up if there was anything he needed to be aware of.

This approach worked well for me and after a few years I was promoted to run the much bigger business in Australia. In this role I was responsible for about half the regional turnover and profit. It was also the sixth largest business unit for the global Petcare business at the time. I made the mistake of assuming the same contract. As such, I was not proactive in reaching out to engage others in the business. At the time I did not realise that this was creating some dissatisfaction with key stakeholders. But it became apparent over time.

When we had a challenging year, with increased competition, this backfired on me. Instead of proactively engaging people in what was happening, I only kept my boss informed, continuing the habits of previous years. I was not deliberately working in an independent manner, but I was not being proactive in engaging people who had a valid interest in helping me succeed. I therefore found myself having to react to questions and concerns raised by global team members and my responses tended to defend the business or provide a lot of contextual detail. For the first time in my career, people started to question my leadership capability.

Eventually, after some good guidance and coaching, I invited a number of the key global stakeholders to participate in a workshop to help us turn the business around. My team and I prepared well. We shared the challenging business context and the plans we had already put in place to address it. We showcased the things that were working well and highlighted the areas we still had concerns about. We divided into smaller teams and workshopped the issues, asking for advice and guidance. What did the stakeholders like? What did they still have concerns about? What suggestions did they have?

I was amazed at how quickly this session improved the stakeholders' perceptions of me. Before the workshop, key stakeholders were questioning my capability and I was being asked to consider moving back into roles in Human

Resources, a function I had been in before becoming a General Manager. After the workshop, and delivering on the commitments we agreed, I found myself under consideration for larger Leadership roles again.

I summarise my learnings from this workshop as follows:

1. The bigger the business or role, the more important it is to proactively engage key stakeholders so they can advocate for you and support you and the business when things don't go as planned.

2. Stakeholders love to be asked for their advice and input. Prior to this experience, I was reluctant to ask for help, thinking it made me look less capable. I realised that asking people for their advice and guidance makes them feel good and enrols their support in your success.

3. Good preparation is key but authentically sharing the reality of the situation is better than only highlighting the things that are going well.

As I moved into more senior roles myself, I saw these lessons play out over and over again. Many times, I visited a business and spent days with people presenting only the things that were going well. Of course, it was great to see things working and I always enjoyed a good opportunity to see some of the young talent in the organisation. But as a stakeholder, I was always more engaged when business teams shared some of their struggles and engaged me in discussion rather than just presenting to me. It may initially seem counterintuitive, but I have seen it work on many occasions, and from both sides.

I certainly recognise that it can feel very scary to raise concerns or questions. You may feel you are giving people ammunition against you, or laying yourself open to attack. I don't want to suggest that you tell people you can't do your job. What works is spelling out clearly the challenge you are facing, and sharing your insights and the ideas you have. Talk about what is working and where you have been disappointed with the outcomes. Be clear about what you are doing to manage the situation and how you are engaging your team in support. Then ask what you might be missing. Do they have any suggestions that may not have been on your radar? Not only will you share your awareness of the situation, you will demonstrate that you take your responsibilities seriously. Perhaps most importantly, you will demonstrate respect and a willingness to learn from others.

I also came to realise that senior stakeholders don't need to understand all the context to have a good sense of what is happening and how you are performing. Successful leaders will get a good sense from whatever interactions they have with you. They will see your curiosity and drive, they will detect how you deal with pressure, how you face problems, how you talk about your team, and how you interact with your peers. And of course, they will see the results you deliver. They will be much more interested and engaged when you discuss real challenges, ideas and opportunities with them, and they will know if you are purely in 'showman' mode. In other words, pretending everything is fine when it isn't, and battling on alone, is highly unlikely to fool a competent superior and has the potential to leave them wondering if you really understand your business.

Building Internal Relationships

People often ask me how to go about building a network. As an introvert, this is something I initially found very uncomfortable. To me, it also felt a little fake. I have written this section primarily for those who feel uncomfortable networking. If you are one of those people who builds connections easily, you may want to skip this section.

Start with building a list of the key people you want to include in your network. How well do they know you now? Are they positive, negative or neutral about you? How influential will they be for your future development? This should help you to identify who are the most important people to connect with first.

I have always been uncomfortable connecting for the sake of connection. It felt a bit false to me. On the contrary, when I had a meaningful purpose for connecting, I found it very easy. The thing I have realised is that most people will be more than happy to make time to connect and to offer you advice on how to deal with a challenge you are facing, or to share what you can do to further develop your career.

So, my simple suggestion if you, like me, have struggled with networking within your organisation, is to ask for advice. This will build an initial connection. Contact the most critical person on your stakeholder map and say something like, "I am working on my career development plan and would love to get your advice," or, "I am facing this particular situation and I'd really appreciate your insights/perspective." It never hurts to play to their ego a little – something like, "You have been very successful in your career, and I'd really appreciate a little of your time to share with me some of your learnings."

I have rarely seen this type of approach turned down. Once you get to a meeting, you can share a little of yourself and your background and aspirations, then soak up the wisdom the person will share. This will open a door for potential future interactions, where you can share progress and ask more questions. You can also ask them if there is anyone else they would recommend you talk to. They may suggest someone you didn't initially put on your list, and/or they may offer an introduction. You will now be on their radar, and they may even think of you the next time a suitable opportunity comes up.

Another good way to build a network is to participate in projects, particularly those that involve people, teams, functions or geographies outside of your usual work area. This will also help broaden your perspective on the business. During my career, I had many opportunities to participate in projects and to take career moves that involved working with different parts of the business. For example, working on a major change initiative in the US gave me unprecedented access to the Senior team, gave me insights into many different aspects of the business, and ultimately helped me to land my first General Management role.

Peer Relationships

One group we might forget when thinking about stakeholders is our peers, especially when you get to a General Manager or Country Head role, where your peers are likely based in other countries. When interviewing for these types of roles I often find that candidates are very clear about what will be expected of them as leaders of their business, but they don't think about the role they will play on a regional or similar team. No matter what position you are in you will always have a role beyond your direct responsibilities to support your peers and line manager, and it is especially worth reflecting on this when you will be working remotely from them.

Certainly, as a new General Manager or senior leader, you will need to focus for the first six to twelve months on understanding your business and your role. But once you understand your role and have it under control, thinking about how you can support the broader organisation and contribute beyond your direct responsibility will be important if you want to progress further. The same applies as you move into even more senior positions. Especially when you work in different locations, engaging with your peers can be a great form of mutual support and learning. This is particularly important for senior leaders, who can otherwise suffer from loneliness in their roles. Not only will it help you progress further, but building strong peer support relationships will also help you manage your own stress and avoid burnout.

Recognising and valuing differences will help you see what others can bring, even when you have a very different approach. I had a different approach from a line manager with whom I was working for a very long time. This was not easy but neither of us was about to change roles. When I focused on assuming he had positive intentions, instead of focusing on the impact he was having, I was able to find new ways to connect with him. More importantly, I was no longer frustrated after every interaction we had. I ended up working for this person for about nine years, and while it was never the easiest of relationships, I learned a huge amount from him, precisely because we were very different. When I stopped expecting or hoping that he would respond the way I would, I started to see the value in his perspective.

Being a little vulnerable, and recognising that we all have things to learn also helps. I distinctly remember my sister, a Human Resources professional, telling me to play to someone's ego. I was almost affronted at first. I personally try to keep ego out of my leadership and it felt very uncomfortable. But I respect my sister greatly, so I decided to give it a go.

This became a real game changer for me in the way I approached certain leaders, including the one I mentioned in the paragraph above. I realised that my tendency to give direct feedback was not being well-received. When I modified my approach and framed my feedback more positively, in a way that supported my leader's ego, he was much more open and responsive, and our relationship improved.

Expanding Your Sphere of Influence

Most of the context above is focused on networks and stakeholders within your organisation. It is also beneficial to look externally. In these situations, asking for advice may not always be your best option, although it can still be useful depending on the context. Make a list of the key external stakeholders you would like to connect with and the purpose for each connection. What industry associations are relevant to your line of work? How well do you know and understand your customers? Are you well connected beyond the purchasing team to understand the various decision makers in an organisation?

For each stakeholder note down what you want to learn from any interaction, and what you can offer to the relationship. Mutuality is important and there will always be something that you can offer. Customers and industry association members are generally keen to connect and will be interested to understand your business and what you can offer. Do be aware of competition law guidelines, particularly with industry associations. If you are unclear on this, check with your legal advisor before participating.

Once you get into a General Management or Country Leadership position it is also very useful to build connections with key government representatives, media and other influencers who may impact your business. Here, your communications or corporate affairs specialists can provide guidance.

In its simplest form, developing good networking relationships is no different from any other form of relationship building. A lot of the topics that have been covered earlier in the book are equally relevant. Good listening, vulnerability and valuing differences are all great skills that will help with networking. The difference is that the need to manage the relationships with your direct team seems obvious and therefore gets done. Building and maintaining a network can seem less urgent and may get deprioritised. I encourage you not to let this happen. Investing a little time in listening to your key stakeholders, and getting to know them and their needs will help you to understand how you can best support them. Broadening your sphere of connections will broaden your perspective. Considering business from a broader perspective will encourage your critical thinking and will open your eyes to new and innovative ways to do things.

With your peers and with external stakeholders the relationship is as much about what you contribute as it is about what you will get. It is like any good investment. The more you put into it, the more you will get out. Chris London expresses this very well when he says, *"Networking with integrity creates a greater willingness of all parties to be part of a human conduit to serve as energy and resource to one another. Sometimes you will give more than you receive and sometimes you will get back more than you give. It's not about keeping score."*

Networking with integrity is really about building relationships with the real intent of delivering mutual value. It is also about maintaining confidences and respecting boundaries. If you are not sure, ask. It never hurts to contract upfront about how you each want the relationship to work.

There is really nothing magical about stakeholder engagement, except that it requires intentionality and focus. *Unless* you make it a priority, it is likely to fall to the bottom of your agenda and not get done. *When* you make it a priority, you will benefit and those you connect with will benefit.

When it falls to the bottom of your list you may find yourself having missed important insights or opportunities. Hindsight is always a wonderful thing, but it is not always easy to redress. Whether you are connecting internally, to build your profile and support your career development with your peers in a mutually supportive environment, or externally, to broaden your influence, the more you practise, the easier you will find it.

CHAPTER TEN
ENJOYING THE JOURNEY

"Enjoy the journey because the destination is a mirage."

– Stephen Furtick

It is very easy to become focused on a goal or ambition and to spend your time and energy striving to achieve that goal. When taken to an extreme this can mean you forget to enjoy the present and it can start to feel like being on a never-ending treadmill. When one goal is achieved you immediately start to focus on the next, constantly striving. There is certainly no harm in setting goals and having drive. In fact, these things are hugely helpful in making you successful. But don't get so caught up in where you want to go that you forget to make the most of where you are. Life is short and you only get to live it once.

It may seem odd to include a chapter on enjoying the journey in a book about leadership. I personally believe this to be absolutely critical. Pursuing your career progression at all costs may result in great financial rewards but there is more to life. I am not aware of anyone on their deathbed wishing they had spent more time at work. I have heard of countless people who, on their deathbed, regret not having spent more time with their loved ones, and doing more of the things they enjoy. Take a moment to reflect on what you want your legacy to be. I would guess it is more than having reached a certain level in your organisation. Who do you want to impact? How do you want to be remembered?

Enjoying the journey is also a good mindset to have when things don't go as you planned. Life is not always a straight path and becoming fixated on one path or outcome can lead to all sorts of negative emotions when barriers or obstacles come up. Maintaining a positive outlook will help you to make the most of every day, regardless of the circumstances. This will lead to you being more pleasant to be around and will help your team and other stakeholders to want to engage with you. It will also have a positive impact on your personal health and wellbeing. Perhaps most importantly, enjoying the journey will help you to leave a lasting positive legacy on the people around you. Think back to what you defined as your purpose in Chapter One. Enjoying the journey will help you get there in a way that retains relationships and helps you to live a fulfilled life.

It can be tempting to continually have your sights set on the next role, the next promotion. Ironically, this can hold you back from achieving it, and can leave you feeling unhappy in your current role in the meantime. In my experience, when you enjoy what you are doing and relish the learning, you seem to perform better. Opportunities come up that you may not have ever considered.

Conversely, I have seen people who are so focused on the next role that they don't perform well in their current role. Even though they have plenty of capability and potential they limit their opportunities. Regardless of your ambition, setting out to do your current job as best you can will always hold you in good stead for the future. Once you have mastered your current role, expanding your horizons and contributing over and above expectations will help you demonstrate your readiness for promotion... but not if it is at the expense of the responsibilities of your current role.

One thing I have found to be very helpful when thinking about any goal is to measure progress rather than focus on perfection. This can help me keep making forward momentum when things get difficult. I remember when my children were young taking them for walks to climb small mountains. We would get halfway up, and they would complain about how much further we had to go. Encouraging them to turn around and look at how far we had already come would give them the motivation to keep going. I have used this same approach many times at work. The further off a goal's achievement seems, the more helpful it can be to look back and celebrate the progress already achieved. Setting and celebrating small milestones is always useful too.

Career Progression

Another common trap I see people fall into is thinking about career progression only in a linear way – like climbing a literal ladder. They ignore or turn down opportunities that may seem like they are going sideways. In the long run, this can limit their opportunities to learn and grow. I think of career progression much more as a spiderweb than a ladder. When you think this way, it opens up possible new pathways that will broaden your experience base. The broader your experience base, the more opportunities will arise later in your career. This is particularly important given there are fewer roles available at the top. Having a good broad base will keep more options open.

I didn't have a traditional career path. From the age of seven until I reached university, I didn't consider anything other than a career in medicine. Around the time I started at university, things fell apart for me at home. My parents divorced and I found myself floundering. I decided I wasn't interested in medicine after all. I left university and did a few office jobs, then got into sales because a friend of mine was in sales and he had a company car. That looked appealing, although my first sales job was on commission, with no car.

I eventually became a sales representative for a Consumer Packaged Goods (CPG) company and got the company car I had coveted. I found I enjoyed sales and I progressed quite rapidly, getting married and giving birth to my two children along the way. I made my way into Mars, Incorporated as a National Account Manager. I was not particularly career focused and didn't have any specific ambitions. I was driven by three things: I wanted to learn; I wanted to be challenged; and I wanted to make a contribution. If an opportunity came along that met those three criteria, I leapt at it.

I made a lateral move into Human Resources and then took what looked on paper to be a backward step, by moving geographies to the US, into a Human Resources role with less responsibility but in a bigger organisation. I experienced the benefit of the shift from a breadth role, where I had to cover the whole function, to a depth role, where I had to develop more expertise. I spent nearly six years in the US in different Human Resources roles, moving from Generalist positions into more specialised ones. I also took the lead on a large change project. The conclusion of that project was the first time I started to get a bit more intentional about my career and expressed interest in a General Management role.

At first, people were surprised by this interest, but as we explored more, an opportunity arose for me to return to New Zealand as the General Manager. I was hugely excited by this opportunity. It was not something I ever realistically thought I would achieve. And it also gave my two children the chance to finish their schooling in their home country.

From that point, I became more focused on what I wanted to do. I had some success in the role and was promoted to General Manager for the Petcare business in Australia. This was a massive step up. In New Zealand there were about one hundred and forty employees (Associates, in Mars language) and it was really a sales and marketing organisation. In Australia I was responsible for about fifteen hundred Associates and all functions, including Research and Development, four manufacturing facilities, and all supply and demand functions. I loved that role, but it was a real stretch.

I have talked in previous chapters about some of the big learnings that happened during that time, which was also when my son hit his lowest point, and I went through a divorce, so it was very challenging personally as well. It was not always easy during that time to enjoy the journey, and I questioned many times whether I was in the right place. There is an old Chinese proverb that says, *"To get through the hardest journey we need take only one step at a time, but we must keep on stepping."* This was very true for me. I focused on getting through each day and always on being the best version of myself I could be.

Looking back, I would not have wanted to miss all the learnings those hard times gave me. I would not be the person, leader or mother that I am today if I had. This has in fact been the case for every difficult period I have gone through – definitely not pleasant at the time but full of growth and learning.

Eventually, I took another sideways move into a global Strategy role. This gave me an opportunity to connect directly with many global stakeholders in a more meaningful way and led directly to my next role as Regional President for the Royal Canin business, Asia Pacific, based in Singapore. After a few years, I took another sideways move to France, as Regional President for the Emerging Markets business of Royal Canin. While this was a smaller region, I took this move as a direct step towards becoming the CEO of the business. It was not an easy move to make during the pandemic, and it meant moving a long way from family again. I was based at Global Headquarters and able to engage more with all the key stakeholders and immerse myself in the culture of the organisation.

Unfortunately, I missed out on the CEO role. This was a good lesson for me in acceptance – a topic I am incredibly passionate about – because I was obviously disappointed. I did have other options I could consider but, in the end, I decided that I would stay for another eighteen months to support the leadership transition and would then retire, after thirty years with Mars, Incorporated.

During these eighteen months I picked up some additional responsibilities that further broadened my perspective and made the most of my time. Retirement has enabled me to move back to New Zealand, closer to my family and young grandchildren. I am enjoying doing a bit of executive coaching and writing this book while being able to do more of the things that bring me joy. With hindsight, this has been absolutely the best thing for me. This quote from Douglas Adams sums it up perfectly: *"I may not have gone where I intended to go, but I think I have ended up where I intended to be."*

I share this, my story, as an example of a journey, and to encourage you to be open to exploring different options along your way. Your path will be different. Every individual is different, and every organisation is different. We all have many and varied opportunities and the choices that we make will determine the outcomes. Regardless of the outcome, when you choose to enjoy the journey, you will have a rich and fulfilling career – no matter where it leads.

Balance

Today there is much talk about work-life balance. Balance is different for each of us. And what gives you balance today, may not work next week or next year. Work demands change and life demands change. In fact, I am not sure that balance is what we should be striving for. What is important is to be intentional about the choices we make, understanding the trade-offs involved, and the impact they will have on us and on others. The one thing I do know is that if you are not intentional about setting boundaries around your work, it will expand to fill all your time. Flexible ways of working and our ability to connect online at all hours of the day and night create more options for how to set boundaries.

When you are driven to succeed, to progress as fast as possible, it is easy to forget your boundaries. Given the demands of work, it is very easy to let your personal commitments slide. It is easy to think, "It is just this once, this week, this month," or, "It will get better next year." There will certainly be times when you need to put in extra effort, for example when you start a new role, or during times of crisis, but if you allow it to, your work will fill your life, leaving no time for family, friends or other meaningful relationships.

It is not always easy to juggle all aspects of our lives. I acknowledge that not all industries or all companies are open and flexible about work/life integration. Thankfully, businesses are generally more aware of these needs than they were in the past. But the tension is real and will continue to exist. I tried hard to be available for my children when they were younger, but my work required me to travel a lot. Today, my thirty-three-year-old daughter will say I was always there when she needed me, but not always when she wanted me. She acknowledges that I needed to work, that it was important for my mental wellbeing and fulfilment, and that it brought many financial benefits to the family. That doesn't change her experience of not having me around as much as she wanted. I am not sure that I would ever have been able to be there enough for her but if I was doing it all again, I would definitely make some different choices.

Ultimately, it is important to value your personal commitments at least as highly as your work commitments. If you don't do this, you will probably keep letting things slide. I remember being in a small group meeting in Singapore when I was the Regional President for Asia Pacific. We went over time and got into chatting about a few things. Later, one of the participants mentioned that he had missed his plan to go and spend some time with his elderly father because the meeting ran late. I asked him why he hadn't said something. If he had had another work commitment, he would most definitely have excused himself. Why did he not value his commitment to his father the same way? This example was a great reminder to all of us about valuing our personal commitments.

There will no doubt be exceptions to maintaining boundaries when something urgent comes up at work, or you are faced with a genuine crisis. The same may happen on the personal side, but when you are intentional these will be exceptions and will not become the rule. When exceptions do occur, attend to them proactively so as not to risk either personal or work relationships.

How you set your boundaries will depend on your personal circumstances. I personally made three choices.

1. I planned out my annual calendar with all my regular meetings and work travel and locked in my vacation time. I generally did this in September or October for the following year. If I didn't lock it in ahead of time, I would struggle to find any decent stretch of time without another commitment to be able to take a really good break.

2. I made a priority of my exercise sessions. I booked a Personal Trainer and made sure to attend my appointments.

3. I chose not to take short overnight flights, even if this meant travelling on a weekend to arrive at my destination on time. I knew that I could not be present with the energy required if I did not get enough sleep before a visit. NB: when my children were younger (and I was younger) I made the opposite choice, preferring to maximise time with my kids.

Making these three choices and being open with my team about them, not only helped me to live within my boundaries but also set a good role model for my team. Setting this example allowed my team to feel more comfortable about making good choices regarding their own needs rather than feeling like they needed to sacrifice everything for their job.

Looking After Yourself

When things get challenging or you face a crisis at work, it can be tempting to throw yourself fully into it without taking care of yourself. This may work for a while but over time your results will suffer, and it will eventually result in burnout. And you won't be setting a good example for your team.

When I was the Regional President for Asia Pacific, the business was hit with a major cyber-attack that impacted all our systems globally. This was a challenging situation for the business and, as part of the global leadership team, we went straight into crisis management mode. We quickly recognised that many people were working exceedingly long hours to resolve the issue, creating a lot of stress in the organisation. Within the first week of the crisis, we assigned a couple of team members to focus on care and attention for all Associates. When we looked back on the successful resolution of the crisis, this was one of the key things that the team identified as a major factor.

Of course, everyone had to put in extra effort and hours to get the business back up and running. And this was not a short process – it took several months. But giving the team, and ourselves, permission to take breaks when we needed them was crucial. Looking out for each other and checking in regularly doesn't take a lot of time but can make a big difference to the level of engagement and can help avoid worsening the issue.

This is where listening and vulnerability can be hugely helpful. One of the mantras I have used with my team is: "Look after yourself first; look after your family second; then look after the business." This may seem counterintuitive but when people feel they can meet their own needs and the needs of their family, they are able to bring their full commitment to their work. It is very hard to concentrate fully and do your best work when you are exhausted or worried about something else, resulting in errors or even safety issues.

When my son was particularly ill, I was able to take some time to focus on him – even though I was in a leadership position. I know I was not able to bring my best to the business during that time and was very grateful that my team and my boss recognised this and supported me.

Tough Times

Unless you are incredibly fortunate, you will experience challenges and setbacks in your life. This could be in the form of health issues for you or your family, or you may find yourself struggling to perform in a new position; you may be made redundant or face other career challenges. Life is not always fair or easy. This is why acceptance is so valuable. When you acknowledge and accept your circumstances, you can keep moving forward. Give yourself grace in any situation like this. Step back and try to keep things in perspective.

I was the Regional President responsible for Ukraine when Russia invaded. I was consistently humbled by the attitude of the incredible team there. They were dealing every day with rockets flying overhead, limited sleep, and often no electricity or running water. They were afraid for their families and for their lives and yet they showed incredible courage and resilience.

After the initial period where we focused solely on their safety and wellbeing, they were keen to get back to some semblance of normality. They focused on the business purpose – to make a better world for the cats and dogs in Ukraine – and worked to support their customers. They pulled together as a team and supported each other in new and different ways. As a leader, all I could do was provide encouragement, and remove as many barriers as I could to enable them to perform. I was constantly humbled by their gratitude for every small thing we were able to do.

I could share so many stories of the incredible resilience of people. I have learned that no matter what you see from the outside, everyone has their own story, and we all struggle with different things from time to time. Making the space to listen to others helps them and helps you to maintain perspective for yourself. And in the end, we all need to find our own path. As Friedrich Nietzsche said, *"That which does not kill us makes us stronger."* I also like the way this idea has been translated into an American proverb: *"The only difference between stumbling blocks and stepping stones is how you use them."* No matter our circumstances, we always have a choice as to the attitude we take to them, and how we respond to them.

Last Thoughts

When I reflect on my own journey so far, I am satisfied. I feel incredibly grateful for the opportunities I have had and for all that I have learned. Things didn't always go the way I wanted; I have faced plenty of challenges and I certainly made mistakes along the way. But I have always kept moving forward. In writing this book I wanted to share some of my experiences and learnings in the hope that it may help you to avoid some of the mistakes I made. At the same time, I recognise that the best learning comes from experience. So, make the most of every experience, and if this helps even a little, I am grateful for the opportunity it has created.

Regardless of the path you are on, enjoy the journey! Get clear on what is most important to you and set boundaries that will enable you to deliver great business results without compromising on what is most important to you person- ally. Listen carefully to your teammates and co-workers to understand what is important to them and encourage them to set their own boundaries. Share your challenges, hopes and aspirations. Be real. Set realistic goals and deliver your commitments, consistently.

Celebrate successes and don't forget to look back on the progress you make along the way. Stay open and curious to learn as much as possible. Value others and the contribution they make, even more so when they have a different approach from you. Build relationships across different fields and with people from different perspectives, by listening, sharing insights and seeking advice.

It is not always easy, but doing these things will set you on a path to great leadership and great success, while building strong and enduring professional and personal relationships that will sustain you.

ACKNOWLEDGEMENTS

"No one who achieves success does so without acknowledging the help of others. The wise and confident acknowledge this help with gratitude."

– Alfred North Whitehead

It seems ironic that this has probably been the most challenging part of the book to write. Gratitude and thanks are not difficult concepts, but I feel I owe them to so many. How can I possibly acknowledge all the people who have helped me to get here? And how can I do this effectively?

I will start with my parents, who raised me to be responsible, resilient, curious and open, with a heart for diversity. These values have been the foundation for everything I have achieved. My father passed away several years ago now, but Mum has been a huge support with this book, providing encouragement and guidance, and being my first reader and provider of feedback.

My two adult children, Nathaniel and Beka, are the light of my life. I have learned so much from the gift of being your mother. I am immensely proud of both of you and the wonderful, generous people you both are.

Thank you, Roger, for being my rock and for keeping me grounded.

I am eternally grateful to Mars, Incorporated for the personal and professional learning of the last thirty years. I would not be the person I am today without the lessons learned and the opportunities Mars gave me. In particular, I am grateful for all the bosses who helped guide and shape me along the way: Ellis, Steve, Ishi, George, Alan, Judy, Polly, Andy, William, John, Loic, and Cecile. It would be impossible to list all the peers and team members but a special call out to the APAC and Emerging and Seeds teams. You all hold a special place in my heart. I love being 'retired' but I miss you all.

Many others have been instrumental in my growth and learning. I will call out only a couple here: a huge thank you to Peter Fuda – your direct coaching approach absolutely changed my life. And a big call out to Tess Cope – you encouraged me when I had doubts about writing and have been a source of inspiration.

A special thank you to Paula and Sophie who provided great feedback on the earliest versions of the book. Your insights and suggestions were extremely helpful.

Lastly a big thank you to Deanne, Carol, Abigail and the team at Authors & Co. You have made the process of writing simple and straightforward. Your guidance and support have been invaluable.